children's
ART
judgment

# TRENDS IN ART EDUCATION

Consulting Editor: **Earl Linderman**
Arizona State University

**ART FOR EXCEPTIONAL CHILDREN**—DONALD UHLIN,
California State University, Sacramento

**ALTERNATIVES FOR ART EDUCATION RESEARCH**—KENNETH R. BEITTEL,
The Pennsylvania State University

**CHILDREN'S ART JUDGMENT: A CURRICULUM FOR ELEMENTARY ART
APPRECIATION**—GORDON S. PLUMMER,
Murray State University

**ART IN THE ELEMENTARY SCHOOL: DRAWING, PAINTING, AND
CREATING FOR THE CLASSROOM**—MARLENE LINDERMAN,
Arizona State University, Extension Division

**EARLY CHILDHOOD ART**—BARBARA HERBERHOLZ,
California State University, Sacramento
Extension Division

# children's ART judgment

## a curriculum for elementary art appreciation

Gordon S. Plummer

*Murray State University*

WM. C. BROWN COMPANY PUBLISHERS

Dubuque, Iowa

242620

*To Wanda, Alison, Nicholas, and David*

We can therefore predict with some certainty that a child who has been exposed to inferior, unformed and unauthentic . . . material for many years will inevitably perceive the inferior as normal. . . . On the other hand, if we want to nurture a more exacting norm in the child from the beginning we must offer him only exacting visual nourishment and he should be exposed to superior examples to such an extent that he will be completely filled with them, for unavoidably in his daily life he will constantly meet with the inferior.

Wolfgang Metzger, "The Influence of Aesthetic Examples,"
in *The Education of Vision*, edited by Gyorgy Kepes.

# contents

# preface

This book on the subject of children's art judgment is divided into two main parts. In any examination of the question of art judgment, criticism, and appreciation by children, the *why* and the *how* must be considered.

The intent of this book is to encourage and develop the essential skills and resources for providing judgment, criticism, and appreciation in elementary-school classrooms. This text is planned particularly for the "classroom teacher." This person may be an experienced teacher or may be one who is preparing to teach. It is deliberately designed to allow maximum freedom for the individual teacher to plan such an offering. There are many "how-to-do-it" books on the market, and one eminent educator has suggested that these books imply that there may be teachers who don't know "how-to-do-it." This book, therefore, is designed merely as a starting point, for it is the writer's belief that there are many teachers who will know exactly how to do it. What is needed is a text which will suggest the basic philosophical rationale for the insertion of such a program into the elementary curriculum, together with some effort to provide sources of information and ways in which the information can be used. The two sections of the book, then, are planned as follows.

**1. The *why* of children's art judgment.** Art is a visual language and also a means of expression and communication. In any educational sequence, children learn facility in oral and verbal language. Nowadays, it is also accepted by most educational systems that there is a concomitant need for children to learn facility in visual expression, hence, the generally accepted inclusion of a practical art period in most elementary programs.

What is *still lacking* is a marriage of the two disciplines: *the making* of art with the *criticizing, appreciating,* and *judging* of it. The first sections of this book deal with this area. A review of recent research and the general philosophies of aesthetic education suggests the reasons for the *why* of children's art appreciation. Further sections deal with the teaching of art history and also with recent curriculum developments in various school systems. Additionally, some recent projects in various public school systems are reported on, and the questions which relate to this kind of experimentation are left open for the reader to ponder. There then follow some suggestions concerning the general nature of a curriculum in the area for which this book is designed.

**2. The *how* of children's art judgment.** This is based upon what is already known of the activities of the art critic. These might be suggested as the following:

*a) The what.* The identification of the work and the name of the artist.
*b)* To describe the work:

    *The how.* The style of the painter or school and the medium in which the work is carried out.

    *The when.* The date of the work, its chronological and sequential position.

*The why.* The influences that operated upon the artist when he was working on the example given. The viewpoint expressed by the artist in the work.

c) Judgmental comment:

A *liking.* Pleasure, happiness, admiration for the work.

A *disliking.* Sadness, displeasure, anger, irritation at the work.

The work of the  ritic, when summarized in this way, becomes an activity that can be presented effectively to elementary-age students. It is true there are many mature and high-level aesthetic judgments made by the professional art critic that are impossible for an elementary-age child. However, we can begin to inculcate the kinds of preferences and judgmental decisions that may one day produce such a person. In the section that deals with this activity, the background information on art is presented in various sections in a clearly recognizable fashion. Sections on the art elements, the function of design, the subjects of art, the ways in which the artist works, and the feelings that the viewer may have when confronting the art object are all presented sequentially. Following each of these sections is a suggested syllabus of work for grades one through six which would cover each of these art topics. In each case there is a clearly defined link with the practical work of the students in art. Following these two main sections is the additional information necessary for both student and teacher to indulge in the critical activity: a basic art vocabulary of useful art words and a bibliographical contribution which may be loosely divided into visual and verbal information. Under the section for visual sources are included films, filmstrips, slide supplies, and film loops. Under verbal information is presented a bibliographical list of books, journals, periodicals, and other publications. There is also a list of suitable publishers.

It is hoped that this book will be adopted both as a reference book for the practicing teacher and also as a course text for some art teacher-training courses in institutions of higher education. Many courses in art education have done little or nothing in recent years to include art criticism or an art-appreciation component into the *teacher preparation.* This book hopes to redress the balance in this respect.

# a background 1
## of vital information

### Art Appreciation

Hundreds of thousands of words have been written on the subject of art appreciation. Many attempts have been made, with varying degrees of success, to foster it in our public schools. In the early 1900s, the "picture-study" approach was common. The teacher would show reproductions of master paintings and would explain the biographical and factual details relating to the works, but there was little individual perception by the students of the elements that made up the visual quality of such works. As Fred Schwartz has phrased it, "The art appreciation of forty years ago stifled the creativity of the individual child."[1] John Dewey, in his book *Art as Experience*,[2] describes the characteristics of an object that is, or could be, considered aesthetic. He describes what he calls the "enjoyment characteristic," and he goes on to list the factors that determine anything which can be called an experience of this type. One thing of which Dewey is explicit is his determination of an aesthetic experience as being high above the mere perception threshold. Viktor Lowenfeld has stated that appreciation must allow for questions of taste, but cultural changes and fashion have marked effect upon this.[3] It is suggested that there has been, in fact, no genuine history of art but, rather, historians who have selected art objects as typical of a period (but only in their view). In more recent books the question has been posed as to whether we need to distinguish between aesthetic experience and good taste.[4]

Similarly, Hurwitz and Gaitskell state that there are various approaches to this problem.[5] In developing taste in the fine arts, the sporadic study of "famous works" of "great artists" is a pseudoliterary study. This, however, does not always develop

1. Fred B. Schwartz, *Structure and Potential in Art Education* (Waltham, Mass.: Ginn-Blaisdell, Inc., 1970), p. 358.
2. John Dewey, *Art as Experience* (New York: Capricorn Books, G. P. Putnam's Sons, 1958), p. 57.
3. Viktor Lowenfeld and W. Lambert Brittain, *Creative and Mental Growth* (New York: Macmillan Co., 1970), pp. 317-20.
4. Chandler Montgomery, *Art for Teachers of Children* (Columbus, O.: Charles E. Merrill Publishing Co., 1968), pp. 10-11.
5. Al Hurwitz and Charles D. Gaitskell, *Children and Their Art*, 2nd ed. (New York: Harcourt Brace Jovanovich, Inc., 1970), pp. 6, 8-9.

the child's visual vocabulary. They suggest that there is a lack of recent research as to how critical perception relates to the growth levels of children. Some authors would disagree, as the following section indicates. There is, indeed, quite a good deal of recent research which suggests ways in which the problem may be tackled. Schwartz denies the need to return to the "appreciation stage."[6] He suggests that teachers know children develop far greater interest when *participating* in art activities, and he believes there is little meaningful learning in the mere literary application of standards for "appreciating" art. June McFee distinguishes between aesthetic judgment and aesthetic response.[7] *Aesthetic judgment*, according to Ms. McFee, is the kind of qualitative reply which an individual makes to aspects of a work of art, beyond mere recognition. *Aesthetic response*, on the other hand, may be a mere perception and a response of pleasure or displeasure to the formal qualities and the elements of the work in view. The aesthetic response, then, however low-level it may be, can be increased in capacity and, in turn, will lead to a standard of aesthetic judgment.

The question of taste, therefore, may develop in a person largely as a result of his living within a certain culture. Group standards and attitudes are customarily the main sources of the development of taste. This is commonly heard in the expression, "I know what I like." This statement shows that the individual has developed an unconscious preference without having a true realization as to why such a preference developed. Some recent research experiments have attempted to counteract what is known as the response "set." This is done by the development of a kind of critical objectivity toward art, and it may arise by the understanding of the simpler forms of interrelationship in elements of design. R. C. Niece has stated that art education is under attack, not because anyone is especially against it, but because no one is especially for it.[8] He describes the "typical" art-appreciation class showing color slides, and he goes on to state that if students never receive any worthwhile instruction in the art of selecting, arranging, or organizing formal elements, they will do these things on a purely hit-or-miss basis. The current concern over environmental quality of our surroundings was possibly foreseen in the *Report of the Commission on Art Education*.[9] In summing up their findings, the Commission described the meaning and significance for education in art. They believed that the field of art education should be concerned with the individual's creation and the study of artifacts as objects of value. This would include the tradition of art as well as images of our own time. The Commission suggested that teachers of art need to be immersed in the tradition of their artistic heritage. Edwin Ziegfeld, in the same work, described the (then) current scene as one of insensitivity to visual aspects of our environment. Ziegfeld stated bluntly that the most affluent society in the world cannot afford attractive surroundings and moreover does not seem to care.[10]

## What Research Has Shown

Research in art education and the nature of aesthetic and perceptual development goes back a long way. In the twenties, a German philosopher, Gustav Britsch,

6. Schwartz, *Structure and Potential in Art Education*, p. 119.
7. June McFee, *Preparation for Art*, 2nd ed. (Belmont, Calif.: Wadsworth Publishing Co., Inc., 1970), p. 7.
8. R. C. Niece, "Art Is Fun?" *Art Education* [Journal of the NAEA] 20, no. 5 (May 1967): 25-26.
9. Jerome J. Hausman, ed., *Report of the Commission on Art Education* (Washington, D.C.: National Art Education Association, 1965).
10. Edwin Ziegfeld, "The Current Scene," in *Report*, p. 7.

together with his colleagues Conrad Fiedler and Henry Schaefer-Simmern, developed the theory of figure and ground. The book *The Unfolding of Artistic Activity* was published in 1947.[11] In the thirties much research was done in England by Sir Cyril Burt; there was other research during the years 1936 to 1946 by Thomas Munro, with his colleague Betty Lark-Horowitz, at the Cleveland Museum of Art. These early experiments sought to establish the "high art achiever." In so doing, however, the researchers began to develop theories as to the nature of originality,

11. Henry Schaefer-Simmern, *The Unfolding of Artistic Activity* (Berkeley, Calif.: University of California Press, 1947).

**Figure 1.1.** Figures 42 and 45 from Henry Schaefer-Simmern's *The Unfolding of Artistic Activity,* pages 70 and 74. Originally published by the University of California Press; reprinted by permission of The Regents of the University of California.

self-expression, and what later came to be grouped under the heading of "creativity." A more recent publication, *The Experimental Psychology of Beauty* by C. W. Valentine, provides us with a very detailed listing of tests from 1900 to the present day, including tests in England, Australia, and the United States.[12]

During the 1960s in this country, the increase in federal funding for educational research gave a tremendous impetus to researchers in matters pertaining to art education. Though these research studies sought information on different subjects, only now are many of the findings becoming crystallized under the generic heading of what might be termed "an aesthetic measurement." One of the earlier research projects of the 1960s was carried out by Irvin L. Child of Yale University.[13] In this study with elementary and secondary schools in the state of Connecticut, the entire elementary school population were tested for their response preferences to pairs of slides. Directions were given which carefully avoided any value judgment likely to influence the choices. The results, as given by Child, suggest that the lower elementary grades choose the "poorer" art work; that aesthetic sensitivity improves with grade level; that this may be improved with experience and/or training. A later study by Child with college-level subjects gave positive correlation between aesthetic sensitivity and art experience.

Paralleling this research is the work of Frank Barron in the nature of creativity. He tested groups for their reactions to preferences for works of art.[14] He found

12. C. W. Valentine, *The Experimental Psychology of Beauty* (New York: Barnes and Noble, Inc., Social Science Paperbacks, SSP 34, 1962).

13. Irvin L. Child, *Development of Sensitivity to Aesthetic Values*, USOE Coop. Research Project No. 1748 (New Haven, Conn.: Yale University, 1964).

14. Frank Barron, *Creativity and Psychological Health* (New York: Van Nostrand Co., 1963), pp 184-87.

**Figure 1.2.** *Barron-Welsh Art Scale,* figures 20 and 28. *Above:* Like. *Right:* Dislike. Reproduced by special permission from *The Welsh Figure Preference Test* by George S. Welsh, Ph.D. Copyright 1949. Published by Consulting Psychologists Press Inc.

that the "artist" preferred complex asymmetrical figures to simple symmetrical ones. These differences were so distinct that he could distinguish two separate groups of people from the scores that they made. He developed a test instrument, derived from the original *Welsh Figure Preference Test,* which was known as the *Barron-Welsh Art Scale.*[15] This gives some reliability in testing for the "artistic" and "nonartistic" reactions to figure preference. Later work by Barron measured differences in aesthetic preference for reproductions of works of art. He found that the nonartistic subjects rejected unnatural and mysterious types of work, whereas the artistic people approved unusual or primitive or experimental examples.

The state of Iowa has a long tradition in the psychology of art and its study. Norman C. Meier spent nearly ten years at Iowa State University in developing tests, some of which are still in use. More recently, Brent Wilson at the University of Iowa carried out an experimental study designed to alter the perception of paintings by fifth- and sixth-grade children.[16] To do this he showed thirty-four slides of some twenty paintings. He tested these reactions before and after a series of lessons given on the subject of Picasso's painting *Guernica.* As a control group he used a nearby school's fifth- and sixth-grade classes which did *not* receive the series of lessons on Picasso's work. A significant difference was found between the two groups when the test was applied afterwards. The group which had received the teaching on Picasso had gained in the usage of certain perceptual terms at the expense of literal ones.

**Figure 1.3.** *Meier Art Judgment Test Number 1,* figure 77. *Left:* Correct. *Right:* Incorrect. Reproduced by courtesy of the Bureau of Educational Research and Service, The University of Iowa.

15. *The Welsh Figure Preference Test* in *The Barron-Welsh Art Scale Manual* (Palo Alto, Calif.: Consulting Psychologists Press, 1959).
16. Brent G. Wilson, "An Experimental Study Designed to Alter 5th and 6th Grade Students' Perception of Paintings," *Studies in Art Education* 8, no. 1 (Autumn 1966): 31-42.

**Figure 1.4.** Pablo Picasso. *Guernica.* 1937, May-early June. Oil on canvas. 11'5 ½" x 25' 5¾". Collection, The Museum of Modern Art, New York. On extended loan from the artist.

6

**Figure 1.5.** Figure 4M, page 303, in *Children's Drawings as Measures of Intellectual Maturity* by Dale B. Harris. Reprinted by permission of Harcourt Brace Jovanovich, Inc., publisher.

All this, of course, is in line with Piaget's findings which are well known to all educators.[17] These findings show that the child's spatial intuition develops from concrete to abstract operations as he becomes more aware of space and objects within it. The young child, Piaget observed, needs action in order to visualize. For example, a cylinder must be "cut" or a slack knot "tightened" before the child can visualize clearly what is happening. The 1926 Florence Goodenough *"Draw-A-Man" Test* was further developed by Dr. Dale Harris in his 1963 book which investigated the drawings made by children as measures of their intellectual maturity.[18] It was found to be useful for ages between four and twelve years, but it lost its usefulness when the children reached the Piaget "concrete operations stage." Another researcher, Gordon L. Kensler at the University of Oregon, tested the effects of perceptual training upon individual differences in ability to learn perspective drawings.[19] He tested six classes of seventh-graders and found that although there were no highly significant results, training seemed to be better than no training. A more concrete result was obtained by Richard Salome when he tested the effects of perceptual training upon the two-dimensional drawings of children.[20] He found that with visual information and greater perception, the children were able to increase the visual content of their drawings.

In September 1968, Harold McWhinnie published the results of a learning experience on the preference for complexity and asymmetry by fifth-grade children.[21] He tested a group of fifth-graders, using the *Welsh Figure Preference Test* already mentioned, a figure drawing test, the *Embedded Figures Test* and the *Barron Art*

17. Jean Piaget, *The Child's Conception of Space* (London: Routledge and Kegan Paul, Ltd., 1956), p. 244.
18. Dale B. Harris, *Children's Drawings as Measures of Intellectual Maturity* (New York: Harcourt, Brace Jovanovich, Inc., 1963), p. 7.
19. Gordon L. Kensler, "The Effects of Perceptual Training and Modes of Perceiving Upon Individual Differences in Ability to Learn Perspective Drawing" (doctoral dissertation, University of Oregon, 1965).
20. Richard Salome, "The Effects of Perceptual Training on the Two-dimensional Drawings of Children" (doctoral dissertation, Stanford University, 1964).
21. Harold James McWhinnie, "The Effects of a Learning Experience Upon the Preference for Complexity and Asymmetry in 5th-grade Children," *Calif. J. of Educ. Res.* 19, no. 4 (September 1968): 183-89.

*Slide Test.* Perceptual training was given so as to resist the "set" toward simplicity/ symmetry. One test given seemed to indicate an increased preference by girls for complexity in art works. However, there was no significant finding in the case of the boys. W. A. McElroy has carried out cross-cultural research in Australia, test-ing the figure preferences of aborigines.[22] No evidence was found of the existence of a general "good taste" level.

What, then, does all this suggest? During the 1960s there was a tremendous amount of research carried out. Much of it had questionable value because it oftentimes sought to measure some minute fragment of human behavior. Out of the welter of results, however, there is just beginning to emerge something concrete— *that exposure to art and working on art projects do increase aesthetic sensitivities* (as art teachers have always suggested). We are beginning to consider the effect of learning as well as the effect of personality in the matter of taste. McWhinnie has observed a high correlation between aesthetic preference for geometric or abstract drawings and preferences for reproductions of art works.[23] People who have had training or experience in art seem to prefer the more asymmetrical figure, whereas those who do not have this experience prefer simplicity and symmetry. One of our crucial problems at this time is to determine the language that we must use between one research study and another. What one researcher calls "aesthetic judgment" another researcher may term "aesthetic preference," and yet the terms may not mean exactly the same thing.

### School and Art Museums: A Common Interest?

A recent issue of *Art Education* devoted almost the entire content to an examina-tion of the role of the art museum in art education.[24] Harry S. Parker III, a director for education at the Metropolitan Museum of Art in New York, suggests, somewhat irreverently perhaps, that the word *museum* has succeeded in meaning nothing very vital to anyone.[25] He believes that the role of the museum is akin to the role of art education in that Americans customarily enshrine both activities in an isola-tion from a real world. This makes both art education and the art museum some-thing in the nature of luxuries and, therefore, commodities which can be dispensed with in time of stress. In spite of many innovative programs which he describes, Mr. Parker admits that the museum still does not affect thousands who either cannot or who will not visit it. The need, therefore, is for an "outreach" which will go far beyond the walls of the institution. Another article, by Professor Irving Kauf-man, supports the view of Harry Parker and points out the paradoxical views by the public of the function of the art museum.[26] Kaufman suggests that museum education has an exacting task ahead, but it is one from which it cannot escape. Other articles concerning the National Gallery and the Smithsonian Institution are included in the same journal. Richard Grove of the Smithsonian Institution sug-gests, however, that schools and museums are very different, and although they have both sworn allegiance to art education, they react in different ways to the

22. W. A. McElroy, "Aesthetic Appreciation in Aborigines of Arnhem Land," *Oceania* 23 (1953): 81-83.
23. Harold James McWhinnie, "A Review of Research on Aesthetic Measure," *Acta Psycho-logica*, vol. 28 (Amsterdam: North Holland Publishing Co., 1968), pp. 363-75.
24. *Art Education* [Journal of the NAEA] 24, no. 9 (December 1971): 4-25.
25. Harry S. Parker III, "The Art Museum and the Time of Change," *Art Education* 24, no. 9 (December 1971): 4.
26. Irving S. Kaufman, "The Promise of Contradiction," *Art Education* 24, no. 9 (December 1971): 13.

problem.[27] The *museum* educational style is not the *school* educational style. Many of the contributors to this issue of *Art Education* had been participants in an earlier series of conferences called under the auspices of The Institute for the Study of Art in Education. Dr. Jerome J. Hausman of New York University, president of the ISAE, was the principal investigator in a study titled *The Museum and the Art Teacher* which was held in conjunction with the George Washington University and the National Gallery of Art in Washington, D. C., in 1966.[28] In this study, a number of teachers took part in an in-service training program for the use of the museum as a resource for the art educator.

Subsequently, the ISAE scheduled other meetings of which perhaps the most important was the conference held at the Metropolitan Museum of Art in New York in 1969. A report entitled *The Museum Community: New Roles and Possibilities for Art Education* was published as a result.[29] The conference participants divided themselves into four groups, each based upon one or two museums. They subsequently met as a larger group and presented their findings. Essentially, the problem for the museum seems to be one of conserving and preserving its collection by going about the day-to-day business of caring for the works, and yet of trying to become more identified with the cultural and educational needs of the population. As for the art educators, they at least came to realize some of the massive problems confronting the typical museum. If the art educators were occasionally critical of museum practice, this was most certainly reciprocated by some museum people. For example, in the Brooklyn Museum it was suggested that art classes for children tend to emphasize self-expression. The speaker, however, suggested that he was old-fashioned enough to wish that there were more training in the disciplines that go into *seeing* rather than into encouraging self-expression.

The sessions concluded with the making of plans for seminars between museum and school people in various parts of the country for the purpose of furthering the aims that they had discussed. Steven Prokopoff, director of the Institute of Contemporary Art at the University of Pennsylvania, was elected coordinator for this program. Two state arts councils have become interested in the sponsoring of museum educator seminars.

## Art History: Teaching and Texts

Dr. David E. Templeton of Western Washington State College published an article in the January 1969 issue of *Art Education* which discussed critical thinking and the teaching of art.[30] He suggests that in the study of the history of art there is a need for contradiction, instability, and even a slight fear of the unknown which will cause the student to think *critically*. He further describes the limited success of a program of this type with elementary students, with certain cautionary comments added. For example, if the discussion of a work of art goes on for too long, it becomes a mere catalog and is therefore boring to the student. Art works to be criticized or discussed must be selected carefully. Some interesting comparisons could be made between works on the same topic, but, again, contrasts can lead to some

27. Richard Grove, "Understanding Your Art Museum," *Art Education* 24, no. 9 (December 1971): 19.
28. Jerome J. Hausman, *The Museum and the Art Teacher,* final report, USOE Project No. 6-2078 (Washington, D.C., December 1966).
29. *The Museum Community: New Roles and Possibilities for Art Education* (1969) Conference Report, Institute for the Study of Art in Education, ed. Richard Grove, then Associate Director, Arts in Education Program, JDR III Fund.
30. David E. Templeton, *Art Education* 22, no. 9 (January 1969): 6-9.

confusion on the part of the students. Mentioning the work of Joshua Taylor, Templeton concurs with his opinion that there is a need for the student to recognize an ability to respond to a work, to describe that response, and to link the response with the physical nature of the work of art.

Fred Schwartz has described the tendency in art history courses to use slides and to cram enormous quantities of information into a relatively short time.[31] He suggests that art history has long been characterized by the use of slides and that this is more than once removed from the work of art. Other researchers, such as Jerome Hausman in a recent paper, have described the difficulties of students who, having viewed slides over a long period of time, confront later, with some surprise, the original art work. The "difference" is sometimes traumatic. It is a fact, states Schwartz, that students in large metropolitan centers are in the best position to enjoy direct contact with works of art. In outlying communities far from urban centers, it is necessary to build a significant collection of exhibition-quality materials. However, even if close enough to a large museum or rich enough to develop a significant collection, there still remains the ability of the teacher to provide adequately the kind of critical study needed.

To offset this lack, Dr. Templeton directed a special study in a six-week summer session at the Department of Art of Western Washington State College.[32] This innovative program entitled "Art History and Criticism in the Public School" was given in 1971, and there were fifteen participants with a wide national and hierarchical distribution (for example, a teacher on a Navaho Indian Reservation in New Mexico and a nun from a Chicago parochial school). The purposes of the program were

1.  to develop a background in art historiography,
2.  to develop an understanding of learning theory and terms of art history and criticism in the public school art classroom, and
3.  to produce instructional units for art history and criticism.

The program was so successful that this type of study has now become an identifiable component in the preparation of elementary teachers at Western Washington State College.

There are many texts for the study of art and its criticism and appreciation. Nearly all these texts have one commonality. They are usually written with the avowed purpose of provoking a kind of humanistic dialogue. Also, they are usually developed as results of years of study, discussion, and teaching in the type of course customarily known in a college as "survey" or "appreciation." Three such works can be mentioned here. They are typical and, perhaps, exemplary: *Encounter with Art* by Reid Hastie and Christian Schmidt; *Purposes of Art* (second edition) by Albert E. Elsen; and *Art as Image and Idea* by Edmund Burke Feldman. In *Encounter with Art* the authors lead the reader through a series of chapters dealing with the way in which the artist works, the processes involved, and the organizational structure of the work of art, to the final four chapters concerning appreciation, judgment, and evaluation. The book is rich in illustration and shows works up to and including the period of abstract expressionism. The authors' avowed intent is to "open a door for looking." They suggest, however, that this is but one door and that there are others. Their hope is that by understanding what

31. Schwartz, *Structure and Potential in Art Education*, p. 200.
32. "Art History and Criticism in the Public School," Art 497, Six-Week Session Special Study, Department of Art, Western Washington State College, Bellingham, Washington.

the artist does, the strangeness of some visual statements may come to be more familiar, and the personal encounter with art will have some reward and satisfaction between artist and viewer.[33]

Albert Elsen's *Purposes of Art* seeks to increase a reader's awareness, understanding, and tolerance of art. Elsen believes that these objectives are best achieved by a familiarity with the history of art. Elsen is firm in his belief, however, that art is not for every man, and his book is written for a public that cares about art. The book covers most of the development of Western art up to and including a chapter entitled "The Artist Today" which includes representatives of Op and Pop art. The illustrations are profuse, but the great strength of this work is possibly as a background reader for the teacher, rather than as a suitable text for students. Certainly it would be inappropriate for an elementary student.[34]

Feldman's book also deals with the purpose or function of art in the preliminary chapters, but then develops a series on the styles of art, and this, together with chapters on structure and elements, leads to a discussion of critical theory and performance in the final chapters.[35] One item of significance is common to these three authors, and Feldman is specific in describing this; namely, all three have developed their philosophical basis, which underlies the writing of their books, through a dialogue carried out over years with students, colleagues, and through discussion with other people who like to "talk about art." These important works, therefore, have been developed through informal conversations and in an unconscious fashion. Many of the ideas and judgments that these authors make are of such an osmotic character that they could hardly indicate, now, the sources from which they were first obtained. This fact has significance for the teacher who wishes to develop a program in the appreciation and critical judgment of art. Moreover, it is a basic educational tenet. As every teacher knows, though, it *is* possible to teach "two pages ahead" of the class; this is, at best, a dubious undertaking. To teach effectively, one must become "immersed" in the subject matter of the material to be taught. This is as true of art as it is of any other subject. Edmund Feldman has also turned his attention to television as a medium for this area of instruction. A new National Instructional Television film series, "Images and Things," has now been produced as a telecourse on video tape recordings.[36] The time for each segment is thirty minutes. The course relates all kinds of everyday objects, art historical source materials, matters of environmental concern, design and consumerism, and, most importantly, the development of criteria of "taste." It is produced for use mainly by nonspecialists in art education, and it is designed to relate interdisciplinary activities.

### Recent Curriculum Developments

George Herskovits of the New York City Board of Education ran a humanities program in the New York City schools in 1966. This program attempted to design experience-oriented art teaching. A TV project "The Role of Art in the Human-

33. Reid Hastie and Christian Schmidt, *Encounter with Art* (New York: McGraw-Hill Book Co., 1969), p. 439.
34. Albert E. Elsen, *Purposes of Art* (New York: Holt, Rinehart and Winston, Inc., 1967), p.v.
35. Edmund B. Feldman, *Art as Image and Idea* (Englewood Cliffs, N.J.: Prentice-Hall, Inc., 1967), pp. 444-98.
36. "Images and Things," Edmund B. Feldman, Director, Video Tape Recorded Series for National Instructional Television, Bureau of Audio Visual Services, Indiana University, Bloomington, Indiana.

ities" was envisaged.[37] The concepts were expressed in terms of human needs; for example, "seeing the way it is," or "how feelings look," or "the shape of light."

In 1967 were established the regional and educational laboratories of which CEMREL (The Central Mid-Western Education Laboratory) of St. Ann, Missouri, is now the only one in existence. This is a private, nonprofit corporation supported in part by funds from the Office of Education and in part by private endowment, typically, that of the John D. Rockefeller III Fund. One of the principal interests of this laboratory has been the development of an aesthetic education curriculum. The idea for such a program was established jointly by CEMREL and the Ohio State University in spring 1967. By the autumn of 1967, CEMREL had assumed full sponsorship for the project. In March 1969, CEMREL conducted a preconference seminar in cooperation with the National Art Education Association in New York City. The purpose of the seminar was to review and advance the current positions on aesthetic education and to discuss their implications for curriculum development. As a result of this seminar, four papers were published:

*Education and Aesthetic Method* by Nathaniel L. Champlin.
*Aesthetic Education in Social Perspective* by Francis T. Villemain.
*The Year Two Thousand and Aesthetic Education* by Ralph A. Smith.
*Alternate Conceptions in Aesthetic Education* by David W. Ecker.

Champlin suggested that the range of possibilities for aesthetic method is enormous. Indeed, he would argue that a way of life is itself a case of aesthetic method. Villemain draws an account of our aesthetic condition and the aesthetic dimension of experience. He considers this a challenge to educational inquiry and practice, and he, in common with Champlin, considers that it may grow out of the history of American civilization. He sees it as a challenge to express in thought the product of what de Tocqueville called the "American Experiment with Democracy." Ralph Smith suggests that an examination of American values for the year 2000 cannot overlook the probable upgrading of the aesthetic elements. Carrying the analogy further, Smith suggests that futurism in aesthetic education becomes something of an observation satellite that provides data for the decisions that must be made in educational programs for the future. David Ecker outlines the essentially monolithic model of curriculum theory, which has always been the major factor in American education. He suggests that this method for large-scale innovation requires a commitment on the part of large numbers of educators at all levels, and he sees this at once as both a strength and weakness. Ecker suggests that before we commence one more large-scale educational innovation, we might seek an alternative strategy or approach which would allow individuals at all levels to commit themselves to some aspect of the program without being committed to the totality. He also considers that such an alternative strategy would provide for continuous evaluation.

In February 1970, CEMREL published *Guidelines: Curriculum Development for Aesthetic Education*, edited by the late Manuel Barkan together with Laura H. Chapman and Evan J. Kern.[38] The authors correctly point out the basically contradictory situation in the schools concerning aesthetic education. On the one hand, schools attempt to provide such an education and seem to exhibit greater

37. George Herskovits, in *Exemplary Programs in Art Education*, ed. Stanley Madeja (Washington, D. C.: NAEA, 1969), p. 39.
38. Manuel Barkan, Laura H. Chapman, Evan J. Kern, eds., *Guidelines: Curriculum Development in Aesthetic Education Program* (St. Ann, Mo.: CEMREL, Inc., 1970).

desire to do so; but on the other hand, they are handicapped by very limited conceptions as to the components of aesthetic education. Many of these programs are merely cultural additions to the more usual instruction. *Guidelines* attempts to set out, in an unambiguous manner, the necessary information to create a genuine aesthetic education curriculum. In designing units of instruction, the editors developed a thesaurus of terminology and curriculum sentences which apply to all the arts: dance, literature, the visual arts, music, etc. The curriculum guidelines have been extensively tested in the schools surrounding the area of CEMREL and currently are being tested in other states.

The White House Conference on Children was held in December 1970 in Washington, D. C.[39] This placed considerable emphasis on multidisciplinary and multimedia approaches to aesthetic education. There were many participants representing all aspects of children's interests. Several recommendations sent by the conference to the White House hold promise for aesthetic education.

In 1971 the New York State Board of Regents revised its regulations for the education of students in grades one through eight in the New York State public schools.[40] It specifically included music and visual arts in the list of subjects that are mandatory. The Michigan Art Education Association has now developed a Professional Standards Commission to participate directly in the improvement of art education in the state of Michigan,[41] while in Ohio at the state level, consideration is now being given to the adoption of the CEMREL program in all the public schools of the state.[42]

### Projects in the Schools

The recent publication by the National Art Education Association titled *Exemplary Programs in Art Education,* under the editorship of Dr. Stanley Madeja, lists several art-appreciation programs carried out in various school districts of our country.[43] For example, in Salt Lake City, Utah, a funded Title I Project included schools in the Central Salt Lake City District.[44] Some preparation of teachers and scholars was made, and a TV core presentation around a concept was then given. The follow-up activities, which sometimes included studio and sometimes handling of reproductions of museum pieces, produced some extremely desirable results among the students. Similarly, in Omaha, Nebraska, an experimental class between music and art for ninety minutes daily was held for a period of six weeks in a junior high school.[45] This sought to parallel basic elements common to both areas. Examples given were rhythm, line, color, and the chromatic color chart or the chromatic musical scale. Other items might include more subjective experiences (such as mood). This experiment mainly consisted of listening to music or hearing instruments played and of drawing while this experience was undergone.

39. *NAEA Newsletter* 13, no. 6 (February 1971): 3.
40. "New York State Revises Art Framework," *NAEA Newsletter* 13, no. 8 (Washington, D.C., April 1971), p. 3.
41. "Michigan Art Education Association Forms Professional Standards Commission," *NAEA Newsletter* 14, no. 4 (Washington, D.C., December 1971), p. 2.
42. "Ohio Holds Meetings on CEMREL Curriculum Packages," *NAEA Newsletter* 14, no. 4 (Washington, D. C., December 1971), p. 2.
43. Stanley Madeja, ed., *Exemplary Programs in Art Education* (Washington, D.C.: NAEA, 1970).
44. Ibid., p. 31.
45. Ibid., p. 33.

in art education    VOLUME 1    NUMBER 2    NATIONAL ART EDUCATION ASSOCIATION

**Figure 1.6.** The cover for *Issues in Art Education,* Volume 1, No. 2. Reproduced by permission of The National Art Education Association, Washington, D.C.

In another work, Al Hurwitz has criticized just this sort of thing as "art integration for pussycats."[46] By contrast, the Hurwitz program at the Newton public schools of Massachusetts was described as being designed to teach visual awareness and critical judgment of aesthetic qualities. One hundred and twenty students were used in two experimental groups of thirty subjects for the experimental program and two control groups of thirty subjects for normal sixth-grade art lessons.

46. Al Hurwitz, "Integrated Arts in the Public Schools," *Issues in Art Education,* ed. Gordon S. Plummer, vol. 1, no. 5 (Washington, D.C.: NAEA, 1971), pp. 1-3.

This was carried out for two hours per week for four months. There was a sorting test instrument used, the *Brent Wilson Aspective Test* and the *Eisner Art Information Inventory,* but the results are not reported.[47]

In 1970 the Office of Education created Project Impact, an interdisciplinary model program in the arts for children and teachers.[48] Programs were located in Columbus, Ohio; Eugene, Oregon; Philadelphia, Pennsylvania; Troy, Alabama; and Glendale, California. One of them has been reported upon in a recent issue of *Art Education.* This is the program at the Edgewood School in Eugene, Oregon. This school has 460 students. The project placed art specialists in music, dance, drama, and the visual arts, in addition to the normal school faculty. The specialists led various teacher teams and used many volunteers and paraprofessionals. A program of testing was arranged so as to study performance and to give answers to questions from both parents and administrators. Initial in-service was given to the faculty by the specialists, and following this the planning of modular instructional units for classes. Some took social studies areas as themes, while in higher grades special activities in the arts were developed. The experience is very similar to that at CEMREL, for by the end of the first year there was a universal need to develop a basic set of principles for the construction of a curriculum in the arts. The specialists who had been attached to the school became the resource consultants, and the teachers developed, in their company, the planning and the writing of curricula. At this time, the statement of philosophy developed by this particular school staff in implementing its curriculum includes the following:

> The student becomes highly involved in the learning experience.
> He is encouraged to investigate and learn about the world which surrounds him.
> His ability to concentrate and develop standards of commitment is strengthened, while at the same time he is allowed to take risks.
> He is encouraged to be more sensitive to both people and situations.
> A variety of educational opportunities helped bring about a more positive attitude in the learning activities.

### Related Questions

As a result of both research and program innovation, we are now at the stage where we may ask ourselves some specific questions in terms of aesthetic education.

Donald Jack Davis has written a major position paper on the subject of behavioral objectives. His thesis is that we must identify those aspects of "art behavior" which are educationally valid in order to change the behavior of our students. He asks three very specific questions:

> What is it that your students will be able to do when they have received from you the appropriate art learning?
> What does a student do when he really "appreciates" art which he does not do when he does not appreciate?
> What does a student do who "really understands" art which he does not do when he does not understand?[49]

47. Madeja, ed., *Exemplary Programs in Art Education,* p. 35.
48. Dorothy DeVeau, "Project Impact in Eugene: What Are Its Implications?" *Art Teacher,* vol. 1, no. 1 (Washington, D.C.: NAEA, Fall 1971), p. 41.
49. Donald Jack Davis, "The Implications of Behavioral Objectives for Art Education in the Public Schools," *Issues in Art Education,* ed. Gordon S. Plummer, vol. 1, no. 1, p. 2.

David Ecker has suggested that we need to develop categories of content for aesthetic education. He, too, asks a question:

When the label "aesthetic education" is attached to a curriculum which provides instruction in the arts, what makes the curriculum aesthetic?[50]

Ecker suggests a "package," or "kit," which will set guidelines for the curriculum planner, the teacher, and the student. This kit would

1. attach the most literal and nontheoretical names to items,
2. classify those items with the fewest possible categories for distinguishing them, and
3. make sure that none are excluded that are considered by a specialist to be important.

Dorothy DeVeau, associate director of Project Impact (already mentioned), also poses some questions. When discussing the best way to raise standards of aesthetic education (by producing a populace which creates art) she suggests that decision-making situations arise during these activities. Some of the questions to the participants might be summarized in this way:

Why does this part look strange?
What is wrong with the way I do this?
How I can best express this idea?

Whether or not we can find immediate answers to these questions is debatable. However, the fact that they are being asked now would suggest that we are moving toward the idea that the arts are no longer considered to be "play." As every artist knows, the art process demands careful thinking, a deal of commitment, and the calling into play of all the power and skill possessed by the practitioner. The aesthetic curriculum will place the responsibility for learning with the learner rather than with the teacher.

### Curriculum in Appreciation of Art for Elementary Grades

There have been many suggestions made in the past, both in the typical curriculum guides and elsewhere, upon the topic of appreciation. The important thing, it seems to this writer, is that the teacher be given the prerogative of making the decisions in such a curriculum. What follows, therefore, is but a suggestion in terms of general topics suitable for a specific age group. Some suggestions are made as to the method of inclusion within the total art curriculum. Other items suggest films, books, and other resource materials that are appropriate to the area of interest. However, there is nothing to prevent the teacher from substituting, replacing, or exchanging different segments of the material presented here. Appreciation, like taste, cannot be taught in a formal sense. What we, as teachers, must try to do is show such examples as will encourage our students to appreciate their beauty, and therefore some feeling for taste will result.

The NAEA publication *Art Education in the Elementary School* makes several suggestions relevant to our interest.[51] Opal Oleson and Reid Hastie describe the

50. David Winslow Ecker, "Categories of Aesthetic Content in Aesthetic Education," *Issues in Art Education*, ed. Gordon S. Plummer, vol. 1, no. 2, pp. 2-3.
51. *Art Education in the Elementary School*, ed. Mary M. Packwood (Washington, D.C.: NAEA, 1967), pp. 47-69.

need for perceptual awareness, together with a knowledge of the heritage of art and the aesthetic experiences that can be developed from this knowledge. Edith Henry, in the third chapter of this book, suggests the selection of certain art experiences.[52] She suggests that in order to "appreciate" and "enjoy," the earlier grades could be introduced to various concepts suitable to their level. Suggestions are animals in art, nature in art, and people in art.

In grades three through six, Mrs. Henry suggests the acquaintance with works of artists in other times by understanding the intent and the ways in which the artists used the visual language. This would include the interpretations of buildings, animals, landscape, and people by the arrangement of the art elements within the work. Mrs. Henry goes on to make very specific suggestions for each grade level for the study of these topics and for later participation in studio experiences related to the topics. In a further section she gives examples of suitable teaching approaches in various elementary grades. Examples are given for kindergarten, in which the children are urged to identify with their experiences of natural events. A rainstorm is one suggestion. Grades five and six, on the other hand, should be studying drawings and paintings of specific historical works. Follow-up activities include arranging these in certain configurations:

1. In the analysis of the elements found within them.
2. In the discussion of ideas best suited for similar work.
3. The evaluation of the work when completed.

As one of the later contributors, Dr. Kenneth N. Lansing, suggests, one of the major aims in art education is to develop persons who are not necessarily professional artists or critics but who can make visual forms for aesthetic experiences and appraise these forms with some degree of taste.[53]

## Sequence and Structure

Critical comment to the contrary notwithstanding, this writer feels that there is merit in the sequential presentation of familiar topics. Children will appreciate those things which to them have already an element of familiarity. Children also will quickly develop within a systematic sequence. If the learning sessions are structured in a fashion that becomes familiar to the class and include segments for the child's self-expressive comment, then such comment will come more and more freely. If the student is aware that at a certain moment during the lesson he will be called upon for comment, he becomes more and more ready to make it.

In another way, too, familiarity can help in this process. The lessons should be begun by explaining that paintings are going to be shown. The first paintings chosen should have interesting stories or facts behind them. Student interest is often aroused more quickly by an exciting fact or story which attaches to the work. Similarly, the works to be discussed should be displayed a day or so before the lesson is begun. Sometimes, it is suggested, students should be encouraged to bring one picture of their own choice. However, this may occasionally result in poor examples. The teacher should therefore withhold this choice until the higher grades in the hope that better examples will be produced. In the event of this still being a problem, the teacher might set some guidelines in the making of student choices, e.g., that the work to be chosen for display by the student should be one

---

52. Ibid., pp. 62-63.
53. Ibid., p. 71.

by a named artist and a reproduction of a work on view in some art gallery or museum. Alternatively, it might be suggested that the work to be brought as a student choice should be a reproduction taken from a recognized art magazine.

## Notation and Reference

All students should keep sketchbooks as a part of their studio experience. There is no reason why this sketchbook should not be extended or, alternatively, a parallel *notebook* be kept in connection with the appreciation lesson. This notebook (or sketchbook), then, should include drawings made by the student from slides or reproductions of old masters, and it should include (in higher grades) some kind of analysis of the segments which go to make up the composition of a famous work.

Another method of encouraging student awareness is for each student to become identified with a specific artist. The student can be encouraged to collect reproductions by this person, to talk about them, to study the artist's life and work, and to form some kind of notebook about the particular artist named. A sharing of experiences could follow such an activity.

## Topical Treatments

Another alternative would be for the student to collect different reproductions on a common subject. For example, "The Horse in Art" might be one such subject; similarly, "Artists Look at the Sea" or "Trees in Landscape" might be another.

Figure 1.7.  George Stubbs. *A Grey Hack with a White Greyhound and Groom.* The Tate Gallery, London.

In connection with these topics, it may be added, also, that the student should never be discouraged from making copies of a master work. Indeed, the teacher might decide that this should be an integral part of the appreciation exercise. Students therefore should be encouraged to make copies of parts or complete works of famous artists. One way in which this could be done is to ask them to copy a particular segment of a work that interests them more than the rest. They might have a peculiar liking toward an animal as portrayed. For example, the little dog in *Arnolfini and His Bride* by Jan Van Eyck is often attractive to children. Another similar example is Dürer's *Hare*.

Animals as artistic subject matter are, indeed, most attractive to children because there are so many aspects to which they can relate. The things that animals *do,* such as running, jumping, sleeping, and eating; the physical appearances and peculiarities, such as legs, arms, feet, and tails, or the fatness or thinness of their bodies, together with strange parts, such as fur, wool, long necks or noses, or short legs—all are exciting as subject matter. Children will quickly assess the artist's performance in these terms.

Their own intimate knowledge of some animals is also a judgmental factor. Pets such as dogs, cats, ponies, rabbits, and turtles, or animals such as cows, horses,

Figure 1.9.    Albrecht Dürer. *Hare*. Reproduced by courtesy of the Albertine Library Collection, Vienna, Austria.

pigs, or poultry, are well known to some children. They also observe wild creatures such as squirrels and chipmunks.

Birds are of compelling interest to many children, even in the inner city. Perhaps the obvious freedom is the main factor. Questions occur concerning the birds' choice of a living space, the materials they collect, the preference regarding perching places, and the food that they eat and bring to their young.

These kinds of observational experiences provide the child with a solid basis for judging a work of art portraying a familiar animal. However, the affective factors also can be discovered through judicious questioning. When the children look at the work, they can be encouraged to describe the thoughts that the artist's portrayal of the animal brings to mind. How the child viewer feels, and why, and perhaps the remembrance of familiar animals are all part of possible evaluative discussion.

There are, also, problems that particular pictures may describe. A fierce dog suggests the dilemma of what to do if a friend is in danger. A kitten crying outside appeals to the protective instinct, and a picture may have similar effects. The animal that is hunted or injured or ill-treated stirs humane qualities. These may be occasioned also by an artist's portrayal of cruelty.

Edward Hick's *The Peaceable Kingdom* is a suitable vehicle for art judgment. On the emotive aspects, the child viewer may possibly express delight and happiness or, conversely, he may express sadness in the knowledge that such things do not usually happen in the real world.

## Ways in Which Children Respond to Art Works

There are certain essential basic learning elements in the domain of aesthetic experience: content is one, concept is another, and creativity (a somewhat overworked word these days!) is a third.

Content is formed through meaning given to an art form, and it is a result of ideas and imagery derived from memory and imagination. Children can express feeling about a particular topic only if they have a reasonable background of experiences which are relatable to it. That is why the customary art program of process and product needs to be augmented by awareness of and information about the whole world of art. Rich artistic imagery can only spring from a rich background of experience.

Visual concepts similarly develop as the result of previous experience. Similarity and difference, scale, surface quality, positional relationships, and linear and formal expressiveness cannot be learned *in vacuo*.

Children continually learn how to perceive the world around them as their experience dictates. The interaction of experience upon visual perceptual learning, and vice versa, is a synergistic process. Each enriches the other. Lastly, the knowledge of media and process helps in the perception and thereby the awareness of aesthetic or artistic quality as experienced in relating to an art work. Brush work in a painting is meaningful to children who have themselves worked with paint and brushes. Sculptural qualities are perceived and appreciated more fully as a result of personal experience in creating three-dimensional forms.

The young mind is full of thoughts, questions, and perplexities. When these same ideas and questions, and even some answers, are discovered in a work of art, the experience can be profound. As a probable result, the child's own art work becomes more creative. At first the ideas are nebulous; there is a vague desire to express in some tangible fashion. The resolution of the idea usually comes about through working with some process or material. Many activities that pass as art are, in fact, antithetical. They do not require that children use their creative abilities, and they offer small returns in emotional or intellectual terms. Copying and tracing of figures drawn by adults, coloring-in of mimeographed designs, and similar activities confine the experience. Painting by numbers makes artistic judgment unnecessary. When the art projects are structured through detailed teacher direction, they deter exploration, discovery, inventiveness, and originality.

The *thinking* which accompanies the art experience should be considered more important than the material end product.

## The Validity of Indoctrination

Most children have very meager knowledge and information on which to form opinions of "good" art. Their opinions, frequently, are derived from what they see in halls, magazines, calendars, advertising, and the like. Television has increased awareness, but "quality" experiences, for the most part, are still limited to the educational or public broadcast channels. Thus, these desirable experiences are not yet part of everyday life. Occasionally one still hears children express a dislike for modern art. The conclusions that formed this opinion are often meaningless to the children themselves as well as to everyone else.

Teachers have a responsibility, therefore, to guide the development of taste. Some may be disturbed by the thought that this may be a process of indoctrination of young and highly impressionable minds. Since, however, all education is a process of presenting material that has been chosen by specialists, it is indeed an indoctrination. Teachers present facts for examination by the children who, in turn, form value judgments. The same is true for art objects, and even if the teacher were to refrain from all comment, the children would still conclude something as to quality. The educational process can include the *learning* of what is or is not good art. Certainly this kind of taste is not an inherited trait; rather, it is caused by environmental factors.

Many of these experiences occur in an informal fashion. Questions may arise concerning the purpose, or intent, of the artist whose work is on view. Opinions may be formed on the success, or otherwise, of the artist's work. Comparisons may be made with similar works, and the children may even suggest ways in which a better visual statement could have been made. This kind of indoctrination into the process of visual evaluation can extend into the total surroundings, and opinion-forming may be applied to furnishings, equipment, buildings, etc.

I do not believe that such learnings could be considered a harmful influence upon the impressionable young mind. Indoctrination, in this sense, *is* valid as an educational process.

# the first step 2
# toward appreciation

## The Link Between Exhibit, Discussion, and Student Personal Art Work

If we surround students with beauty, we can hope that appreciation and good taste will result. When the art works are introduced to children, it is suggested that there always be an opportunity for discussion. The slide, picture, or object should be placed at the child's eye level. The questions and comments of the students will provide the discussion which should lead to finding more and more about an artist, pronunciation of the artist's name, where he lived and when, where the work is now, and how it was created. Students should be encouraged to bring material from home or from a library. The discussions may lead the students to find out more about works which are in their school corridors or other classrooms. This discussion should create familiarity with art masterpieces. Each work should be chosen because of the interest it has for children, not adults. Observation and study of the reactions reveal that children often like abstractions and see in them brilliancy of design and exciting colors. When students have the opportunity, they speak honestly and are not worried about how others may think. In this series of topics there always will be an inclusion of a link with the student's own personal art work. It is important that this link be developed and strengthened. There is no reason why the student should not be encouraged to work in the same manner as an artist that he has been studying, nor is it meretricious to make copies of famous works. Any meaningful activity of this nature, provided it is not carried to excess, is legitimate.

## The Elements of Art

Elementary-school-age students (even at grade one) can be introduced in an informal manner to those elements which together make up the work of art. These elements take on greater importance as, with age, the child begins to realize more and more the simplicities and also the complexities that occur in art. The elements of art should be introduced in their several and distinct manners as topics in themselves. The series of schemes of work which follow this section indicate this kind of development.

## Element 1—Line

The most common way of imagining line is that of the mark made by a pointed object when it is passed across a flat surface. However, we should show students that it may also be the edge of a shape or the contour of an object or solid form. We may also see it as a line running through a shape, which gives it direction. Again, it may be considered to be the seen, or perceived, edge of a form. (This is most often apparent in the silhouette.) Once we have established these basic descriptions, we can then go on to elaborate, by the use of various examples, the manifestly different fashions in which the artist uses line. The artist may vary his line by making it thick or thin in stroke, or he may alter its character by the way in which it is applied in terms of its several directions. For example, a thick straight line seems to have great solidity; a thin wavy line indicates liveliness. A line may imply a slow, yet rhythmic, movement. It may imply excitement or calm. It may have great character purely from the way the artist has chosen to apply it. Similarly, the artist can use varying thicknesses to imply closeness or nearness of one object as opposed to distance of another. We will see more of this quality when discussing perspective. Most students will quite readily appreciate the qualities of line. It is, after all, something with which they have had experience almost from the time they began making marks. Even an inky finger on a paper sheet will make a kind of line.

## Element 2—Form

### SHAPE

*Shape* may be defined as a formal space which possesses edges or boundaries that we can perceive. It has length, and it also has width, but it does not have depth. This quality is what we think of as a shape. It is, in two-dimensional terms, a flat form. Possibly the simplest example is the *silhouette*, which in painting or drawing is the form created by filling in the outline with one color.

In perceptual terms, however, the outer contour is not the decisive feature. The *line, thrust,* or *skeleton* that exists within the shape is. This is established by the axis or axes of the figure. For a simple example, one may compare geometric shapes. The axes of a triangular shape are oriented differently from those of a parallelogram.

### MASS

*Mass,* unlike shape, is a form with all three dimensions. It has length, and it also has breadth and depth. It is, therefore, solid and three-dimensional in character. This may appear to be a contradiction in terms when examining certain types of art work. Nevertheless, for the age level with which this book is concerned, we must keep our concepts as simple as possible in order that they may be the more readily understood. Should questions arise from a contradictory example, we can indulge in a fuller explanation. It is important for our students to realize that all works of art have something which is described as "formal qualities." These words are sometimes used by the critic or the artist in different ways. For example, there are such things as static (as opposed to moving) shapes. If our attention is drawn to a shape because of its dynamic quality, then we may have a subtle feeling of disturbance within the work of art. The illusion of depth may sometimes be created by shapes that overlap one another. This, then, is one of the main problems when dealing with formal qualities. In sum, it may be said that mass is created

**Figure 2.1.** Herbin. *Alphabet Plastique*. Reproduced by permission of Galerie Denise René, Paris.

by an illusion when it appears in a two-dimensional work of art. Shape may occur in either two or three dimensions.

### Element 3—Texture

The quality of *texture* in a work of art is that which applies to its surface. The appearance of the surface of the art work can be soft or hard, smooth or rough, shiny or dull, or slick or grainy. Texture is used by the artist for contrast and variety and sometimes to unify different areas of the work. The artist may also call upon the use of texture to portray natural effects, for example, mist or rain in landscape. The effect of aerial perspective is also seen by the softening of the texture. There is, of course, another use of texture by the painter and the sculptor. This use is one in which the texture itself is used as a vehicle of expression. This is seen in the types of paintings which are carried out with large impasto areas of paint, usually applied with a palette knife. The sculptor, similarly, may use the textural qualities of stone, wood, or metal to create a certain effect.

### Element 4—Value

*Value* is seen in a work of art as differences of lightness and darkness. It takes the form of shadows and highlights, and it is often used to create contrasting shapes. Value can be used to express a mood or emotion, and this can be seen where soft shadow is used to create a feeling of quiet and softness. Another case might be in the use of a highlight to emphasize some dramatic quality in a particular part of the work. Rembrandt's *A Man in Armour* is a typical example. Thus we may see the use of value for dramatic purposes in some of the works of the High Baroque and may note softness in the later French romantics such as Millet's *The Gleaners* or in some paintings of J. M. W. Turner. In three-dimensional art, contrasts in value are often produced by the way in which the masses recede or project out from their base line. Sometimes, as in sculpture, the use of light and dark stones or woods create the effect desired. Sometimes recessions or deep hollows in the sculpture help heighten the values and the contrasts between them. We can, for example, note this in the works of Henry Moore. The "form within a form" of Moore's work relies heavily upon the contrast in value that occurs in it. The sculptures of Hans (Jean) Arp, such as his famous *Rhythm in Space*, or the work of Barbara Hepworth, such as *Pelagos*, both exploit the contrasts of value seen with the effects of light upon the smooth, rounded forms. The same idea is given different treatment in the later works of sculptor Jacques Lipchitz, for example, *Prometheus Strangling the Vulture* or *Jacob Wrestling with the Angel*. Here the sinuous interplay of the entwined forms is enhanced by the constantly changing values. Louise Nevelson, some of whose angular bookshelf-like sculptures are supremely rich in relief, evokes powerful visual effects. These assembled "boxes," containing a varied collection of items, exploit the differing values created by these forms within forms. She has had many feeble imitators in college student art work. However, the original ideas expressed in her *Royal Tide V*, for example, are valid as an inspiration to encourage experiments with numerous formal groupings of related objects.

### Element 5—Color

*Color* is probably one of the most difficult and one of the worst-taught aspects of our art programs in public schools. Although there may be some merit in the

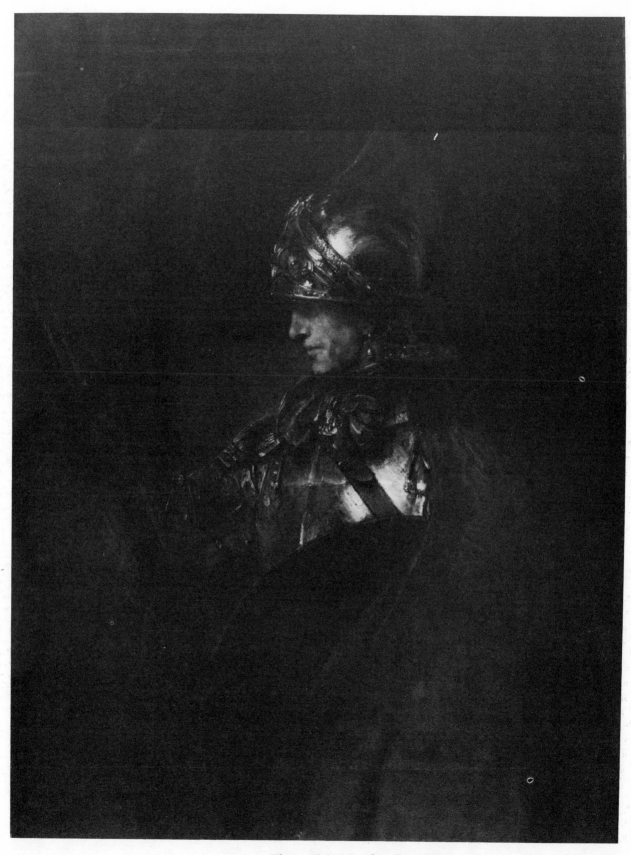

**Figure 2.2.** Rembrandt. *A Man in Armour*. Glasgow Art Gallery

*Page 28:*

*Top:*

**Figure 2.3.** Millet. *The Gleaners.* The Louvre, Paris. SCALA —New York/Florence.

*Bottom:*

**Figure 2.4.** J. M. W. Turner. *Bridge of Sighs, Ducal Palace and Custom House.* Venice: Canaletto Painting. The Tate Gallery, London.

use of the color wheel, this is hardly the point of departure for very young students. Only when the student is ready for such complications should they be employed as teaching aids.

We might begin by talking about sunlight. Sunlight, as can be proved by the use of a prism, contains all the colors of what we term the *spectrum.* This is true of any white light. However, we can explain to our students that when all these colors are mixed in this particular way, each color is cancelled out. When an object is seen as possessing a particular color, it is because some parts of the sunlight are absorbed by it and do not reflect again, whereas others are reflected. If we look at a banana, therefore, we see that it reflects those parts of the sunlight that we have decided to call yellow. Color, then, is one of the chief tools of the artist in expressing a particular effect. It can be used to make for variety, to unify something, to lend an emphasis to a particular shape, or, again, as with value, to express a mood or deep emotional content. We might explain to our students that there are warm and cool colors. The warm colors are usually supposed to be those which contain yellow and red. The greens and blues are considered cool colors.

At some point in our teaching we shall have to refer to color as a combination. This combination is that of *hue, value,* and *saturation. Hue* is what makes one color different from another. As we have already discussed, *value* is the darkness or lightness of the color, and *saturation* is its purity or, in other words, how bright it is to our eye.

We shall also have to enter into a brief explanation of *primary, secondary, tertiary,* and *complementary* colors. *Primary* colors are red, yellow, and blue. *Secondary* colors occur when the three primaries are mixed: orange, green, and purple. *Tertiaries* occur from a mixing of secondaries. *Complementary* colors are the direct opposites of one another on a color wheel or within a formal arrangement of the spectrum.

## A Syllabus on Art Elements—Grades One Through Six

**The Elements of Art**

### Grade 1

*Behavioral Objective.* To familiarize the students with the many qualities of line.

*Presentation.* Show a film such as *Color and Calligraphy.* Discuss the many qualities of line that have been outlined in the preceding section of this book.

*Discussion.* The following questions might be posed to the class. Others may arise, and should these occur, naturally they should be encouraged and expanded.

How does a line vary?
How does an artist use line to express excitement? to express calmness or quiet?
Where can we see lines in nature?

*Summation.* Allow the influence of the examples to show in the children's own work. Have them make "blind contour" drawings of objects. This is done without removing the pencil from the paper at all. It forces the student to keep his eye upon the object which he is attempting to portray, and the connection between eye and hand is more firmly established. It should be a matter of personal encouragement and exhortation to persuade the student that his early clumsy effects will materially improve with practice.

Other examples that might usefully encourage linear treatments would be demonstrated by showing the work of Ben Shahn, for example, *Miners' Wives*. Other artists known for their creative use of line are the Germans George Grosz, as in his *War Cripples* pen-and-ink drawings, and Paul Klee, *The Twittering Machine* and *Song of the Mocking Bird*.

**Figure 2.5.**    Ben Shahn. *Miners' Wives*. 1948. Egg Tempera on Board. 48 x 36 inches. Philadelphia Museum of Art: Given by Wright S. Ludington '51-3-1.

**Figure 2.6.** Bernard Buffet. *Head of a Clown*. Reproduction from Editions BRAUN; reproduced by permission of Maurice Garnier, Paris.

A later example is French artist Bernard Buffet's *Head of a Clown*. This artist has consistently used line, not solely to define, but to add to or enhance the qualities of his chosen forms. Many advertising artists now exploit this same idea in apparel and shoe designs. The "idiom" has visual attractiveness beyond merely defining the form.

## Grade 2

*Behavioral Objective.* To make the students aware of the formal properties in a work of art. To have them distinguish between shape and mass.

*Presentation.* Display some examples of Navaho sand paintings or other American Indian geometric designs which strongly emphasize shape. Have these examples displayed for some days so that the children may look at them and form opinions on them. Have further examples of Eskimo sculptures such as those made from soapstone or walrus tusks. These are examples of the artist's use of mass. Other suitable examples might be the works of Lyonel Feininger—*Gate Tower II, Church in the Market Place,* and other architectural subjects; or the works of Joan Miró; or the later cutouts of Henri Matisse, for example, *The Snail* (1953).

In terms of sculpture, examples of massive form could be exemplified in the *Statue of Liberty,* the Lorado Taft *Blackhawk* statue in Oregon, Illinois, or in *Jacob and the Angel,* Jacob Epstein's powerful alabaster sculpture in London.

If printed reproductions or photographs are not available, the use of slides may be an alternative. These can be either projected on a continuous projection basis or displayed on a windowpane in such a way that they can be viewed against daylight.

**Figure 2.7.**    Sand painting. Navaho Group, showing medicine ledge with sand paintings used in curing the sick. Canyon de Chelly, Arizona. Courtesy of the American Museum of Natural History, New York.

*Discussion.* The following questions may be used as a starting point for class discussion.

How can we recognize a shape?
How can we recognize a mass?
What is form?
How do these things appear to us in a work of art?
Can you discover an example of this in one of the works we have been looking at for the last few days?

*Summation.* The students might be encouraged to work on collages and possibly to use some of the elements they have seen in the examples displayed. Another useful activity might be appliqué, whereby simple cut-out felt shapes are stitched to some other material to provide a pleasing decorative design for some useful object. Another activity which would correlate well with the behavioral objective would be for the students to indulge in simple three-dimensional work, such as modeling in plasticene or clay (which is an additive process) or carving in such things as blocks of soap (which is a subtractive process).

**Figure 2.8.** Dogsled team and seal carved in stone. Sled and harpoon of walrus ivory. Eskimo. Eastern Canadian Arctic. Courtesy of the American Museum of Natural History, New York.

## Grade 3

*Behavioral Objective.* To encourage the students to recognize textural qualities and to be aware of their significance in a work of art.

*Presentation.* For some days prior to the discussion there should be an exhibit of reproductions of the work of famous painters who have used texture. Recent examples might be those of Mark Tobey, Jackson Pollock, Morris Graves, Willem de Kooning, Karel Appel, and Jean Dubuffet. Exhibit, also, reproductions of stone and wood pieces showing use of texture. Possibly sculpture by Nevelson, Nakian, and Lipschitz would be good examples. Try to make clear the reason underlying your choice of these examples for display.

*Discussion.* Questions one might phrase are the following:

What are the different kinds of texture that we see in a work of art?

What kinds of textures may be made with a pencil? a piece of chalk? a piece of charcoal? a dry brush? a wet brush?

How can an artist use texture to add something to the appearance of an object or sculptured piece?

*Summation.* Encourage the class to develop a textural quality in their own work. There may be an overenthusiastic response to this as is common in young students with any new discovery.

## Grade 4

*Behavioral Objective.* To examine the notion of value in chiaroscuro, contrast, etc. *Chiaroscuro* is an Italian word for light and shade. In French it reads *clair-obscur,* and in English *clear-obscure* (unclear). It is generally agreed to mean the balance between lighted and shadowed areas in a picture, and the managing of these shadows skillfully is one of the marks of a good artist. The exemplars of this technique were the artists of the High Baroque such as Caravaggio and Rembrandt. The students, after examining appropriate examples, should begin to perceive how the dramatic qualities of a work of art are heightened and intensified by the use of contrast in light and shade.

*Presentation.* Choose and exhibit some reproductions of Baroque paintings, together with some good examples of modern photography—the work of Caravaggio, Courbet, and the photographs of Josephson and Morse.

*Discussion.* The following questions might be used in this connection for class discussion:

How does a highlight excite our attention?

How does contrast add to form?

When a shadow falls upon the ground, how does it show the ground surface?

How does light help the photographer?

*Summation.* At this point one might encourage the class to indulge in some photographic work, using simple cameras. Any type of camera that is appropriate may be used, and the children should be encouraged to either buy or bring their own. The more simple the camera the better it is for this type of experience. There is one prestigious private institution in this country which has a full-fledged photography program for its preparatory-level students. The students use ninety-eight-cent Rover cameras with great success. A Kodak Instamatic might be another alternative. The teacher should make adequate preparation for such experience by

*Page 35:*

**Figure 2.9.**   Caravaggio. *Conversion of St. Paul.* S. Maria del Popolo, Rome. SCALA — New York/Florence.

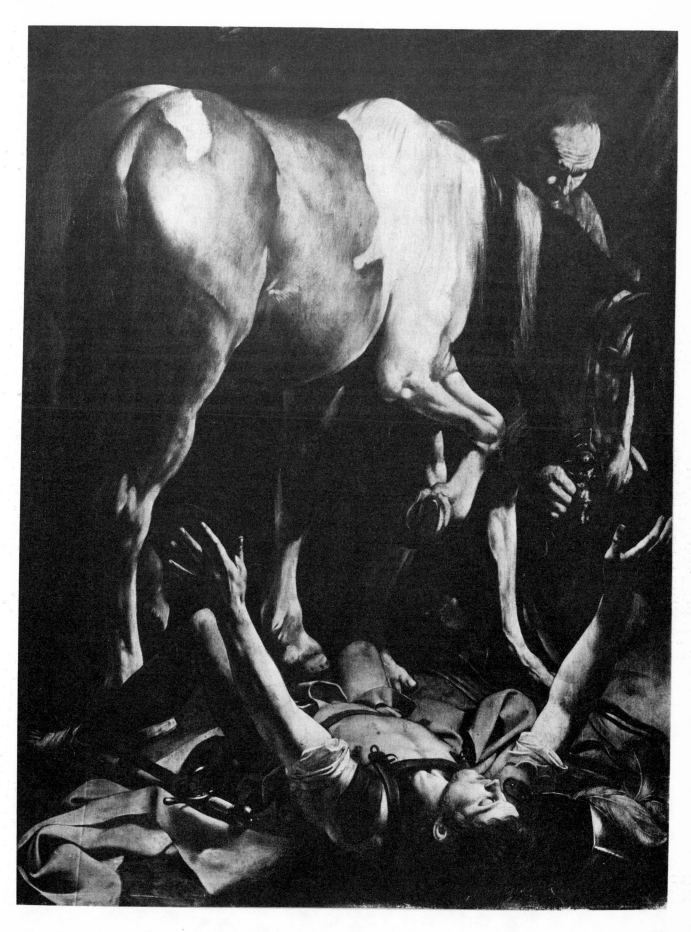

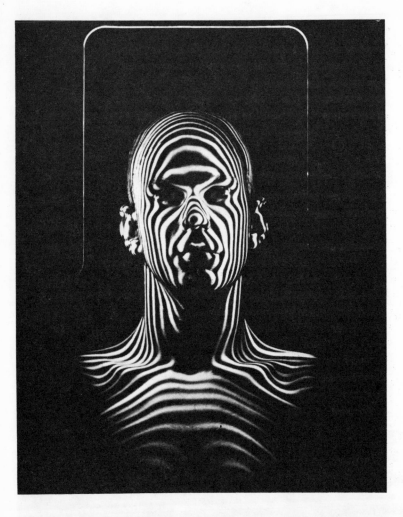

*Left:*
**Figure 2.10.** *Space Age Man.* Ralph Morse, *Life* Magazine, copyright 1953, Time Inc.

*Below:*
**Figure 2.11.** Kenneth Josephson. *Chicago, 1961.* Reproduced by courtesy of Kenneth Josephson.

warning the students in advance to bring the camera with film loaded. They should then be encouraged to create simple contrasts (using value in light and dark) for the photographs they take.

## Grade 5

*Behavioral Objective.* To examine some possible properties and effects of color as it may relate to both great art and the students' own work.

*Presentation.* Try to have on display for several days some reproductions of the works of Renaissance and Venetian painters such as Bellini. Contrast this with some modern works such as Marisol, Josef Albers, Robert Indiana, Franz Kline, and Frank Stella.

**Figure 2.12.** Giovanni Bellini. *Madonna and Child with Pomegranate.* Reproduced by courtesy of the Trustees, The National Gallery, London.

*Page 38:*

**Figure 2.13.** Marisol (Marisol Escobar). *The Family.* 1962. Painted wood and other materials in three sections, 82⅝ x 65½". Collection, The Museum of Modern Art, New York. Advisory Committee Fund.

*Discussion.* Following upon the students' examination of the displayed works, the following questions might be posed:

How does a *warm* color affect our feelings about other work?
Can we find *cool* colors that are used for contrast?
Why do many modern painters use so many primary colors?
Do you like bright, warm colors?
Do you prefer cool, restrained colors better?

At this point the students should be encouraged to discuss more fully the works on display and to express likes and dislikes at some length.

*Summation.* Have the students experiment in their own works with colored papers either cut or torn into shapes. They might decide to use as a stimulus the everyday objects that are around them, in the classroom, or at home. Andy Warhol's *Soup Can* may be used as a possible stimulus, but the emphasis in the student work should not be upon the excessive realism of Pop art. Rather, the work should proceed from the starting point of a known and familiar object to the development of a simple but brightly colored paper shape.

*Right:*

**Figure 2.14.** Andy Warhol. *Campbell's Soup.* 1965. Oil, silk-screened on canvas, 36⅛ x 24¼". Collection, The Museum of Modern Art. Elizabeth Bliss Parkinson Fund.

## Grade 6

*Behavioral Objective.* To have the students become aware of the basic principles of color theory and the terms employed to describe it.

*Presentation.* Exhibit a color wheel. Exhibit some reproductions of famous paintings. Provide a supply of brightly colored silk thread, possibly obtained from a high-school home economics room or from a department store which specializes in sewing activities. Leave the selection of threads on the same table or shelf as the displayed works of art and the color wheel. During the preparatory display period, encourage individual students to try matching the colored threads to colors they see in the color wheel and, later, to colors they perceive in the reproductions.

*Discussion.* Discuss the meanings of *hue, saturation,* and *value.* Discuss the meanings of *primary, secondary,* and *complementary* colors. Ask the following questions.

What is a primary color?
Give an example of a secondary color.
How can one recognize complementary colors in relationship to one another?
What is meant by *value?*
What do we mean by *saturation?*
What is *hue?*

*Summation.* Have the students perform an exercise whereby they will produce a screen of colored silk threads which match exactly the colors of a painting reproduction. This might be done by encouraging the students to provide for themselves a small, colored reproduction of a work of art. This could be pasted onto a sheet of cardboard. A window-type aperture could be cut in the cardboard alongside the pasted-on reproduction. The threads could be arranged across this "window" and taped in series at the back of the cardboard. The exercise can become tedious if prolonged for too long. It can, however, be sustained by some students.

An alternative exercise might be to have students select colored transparent papers or, around Christmas time, colored, brightly decorated materials from Christmas wrappings or similar sources. The important thing about any follow-up exercise which relates to this question is that the student in the sixth grade should be given some fairly demanding activity which requires a closer examination by him of the properties of color.

# additional stages 3 in learning to judge

**What Design Means**

The word *design*, when applied to matters of fine art, has different meanings. The arts of design, however, may be described broadly as the visual arts. In some senses the word *design* may mean the same thing as *composition*, that is, the arrangement of shapes and elements within the total area of the art piece.

The plan or general conception of a work of art, then, described as the *design* is the more general sense of the term as known to us. However, since the last century, this term has become applied more and more to objects which are attractive and well made and are formed for purely utilitarian purposes. We may, for example, talk about automobile design. We may talk about the graphic designer, and we are talking of the man who designs attractive advertising material to be produced by the print media. We may similarly talk about interior design in relation to home furnishings; to fashion design in relationship to those items which are produced for women's wear. However, it would be well with the elementary-grade student to stress first and foremost the use of the term *design* in the more classic sense.

*Design* means rhythm, balance, proportion, and gradation.

## Rhythm

This term refers to the constant repeating of the same elements in a work of art. This may take the form of the same line, shape, etc., which upon being repeated enough times to make it happen in a certain order sets up a sense of rhythm within the total work. The rhythmic repetition of elements may be in the form of lines, dots, gradations of color or tone, or the repetitious use of an element such as texture. Examples of rhythm occur constantly in our daily lives. The ticking of a clock, the noise of running water, and noises made by machines are all typical. Anyone who has heard the noise of highway traffic, such as the roar of passing trucks, has experienced this. There are, however, other examples of rhythm, as in nature. Children will certainly be aware of the effects of the wind upon skyborne cloud formations or the rhythmic bending of trees in a gale. They will possibly have experienced the rhythmic lapping of waves at the sea- or lake-shore; and the seasons of the year have their own rhythm.

**Figure 3.1.** Wang Chien. *White Clouds Over Hsiao and Hsiang.* Scroll. Courtesy of the Smithsonian Institution, Freer Gallery of Art, Washington, D.C.

**Figure 3.2.** Charles Sheeler. *Aerial Gyrations, 1953.* Courtesy of Kennedy Galleries, Inc., New York.

In art, the Chinese have often portrayed the rhythm of clouds, mountains, and other natural forms. Rembrandt's *The Three Trees* is a rhythmic visual arrangement, and the American artist Charles Sheeler has captured the rhythms of contemporary industrial landscape.

### Balance

*Balance* can be a symmetrical arrangement or an asymmetrical one. In a symmetrical arrangement it means that the elements are so arranged on each side of something (even, perhaps, a space) that they equalize each other in emphasis, in strength of color, or in any other way that provides a visual impact upon the viewer. In an asymmetrical arrangement the same thing applies, except that the shapes, elements, or forms are arranged on either side of a central point but at varying distances or in varying sizes. For example, an asymmetrical balance may be obtained by the use of a small object which is colored with a primary (and therefore strong) color and balanced by a larger shape which is colored with a secondary color. The *balance* is obtained, therefore, by the relative amounts of strong and weak colors. This may be done with any of the elements of art: lines, dots, textures, etc.

**Figure 3.3.** Krater. *Death of Actaeon.* Greek, Attic Red-figured. Courtesy Museum of Fine Arts, Boston. James Fund and Special Contribution.

**Figure 3.4.**    Barnett Newman. *Broken Obelisk.* 1963-67. Reproduced by permission of Mrs. Barnett Newman.

**Figure 3.5.** Burgoyne Diller. *First Theme 1962.* Oil on canvas. 72 x 72″. Courtesy of The Art Institute of Chicago. Wilson L. Mead Fund.

## *Proportion*

*Proportion* is the relationship of different things by sizes. During the Renaissance, many painters thought that proportion could be applied to the human figure, just as they thought it should be applied to objects and even architecture. For example, many Renaissance buildings were constructed according to something known as the *Golden Mean*. This Golden Mean was the name given to a rather mystical proportional arrangement, known since classical Greek times, which was thought to possess some aesthetic virtue within itself. When designing the Golden Mean the Renaissance artists usually took the example of a line which was divided in such a way that the smaller part was to the larger as the larger part was to the whole (*AB* cut at *C*, so that *CB*:*AC*=*AC*:*AB*). Another use of proportion was that in which Leonardo da Vinci made his drawing of *Vitruvian Man*. In this drawing he attempted to relate the parts of the human figure in a geometric fashion. In these days, artists and art students customarily use proportion when endeavoring to relate the sizes of things seen for the purpose of drawing them. For example, we may decide that a certain number of "heads" total the correct height for an adult male, or to put it another way, the distance from the top of the head to the chin may be repeated for a certain number of times, and if it occurs in the correct number from head to feet, the figure will thus become a drawing that is "in proportion." Proportion is also used where some kind of rough approximation is made visually. This is often done by holding a pencil at arm's length and, with one eye closed, making approximate visual measurements. These measurements are then transferred, in the same proportion, to the drawing. Thus we may say that the typical door is two and a half times as high as it is wide.

**Figure 3.6.** Leonardo da Vinci. *Vitruvian Man.*

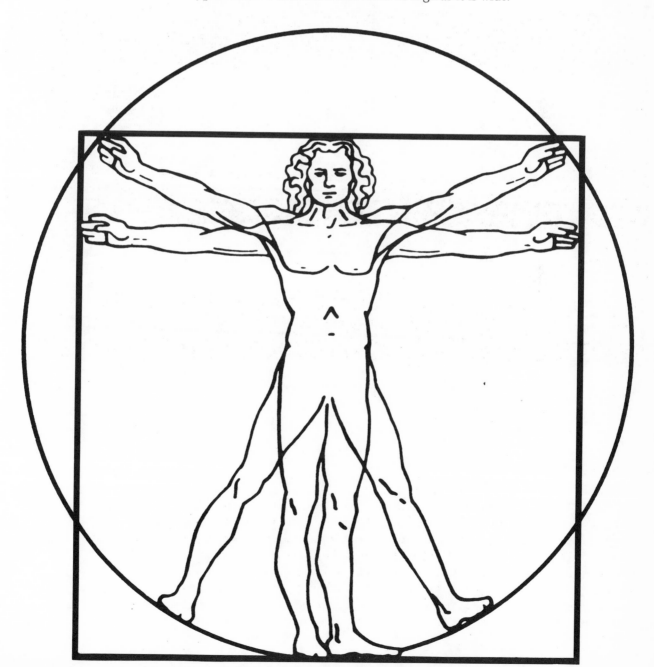

## Gradation

The term *gradation* may be used in several ways, but generally it refers to the development of something that seems to lead toward a climax or high point. When color is gradated, it implies that the color gradually changes its hue, its saturation, or perhaps its value. In terms of light and shade, a painting or other work

**Figure 3.7.** Joseph Stella. *Brooklyn Bridge*. Oil on canvas. 84 x 76 inches. Yale University Art Gallery. Collection of the Société Anonyme.

may gradually darken or, perhaps, lighten and lead the eye of the viewer in a successive gradation toward the important point within the work to which the eye should be drawn for completion. The term *gradation* can be used in many ways, but in general, the first definition, that which leads to a high point, is the one that elementary-grade students will most easily understand. When developing technical problems, for example, the application of a *wash* in watercolor, the term *gradation* may be used, and its immediate effects will be readily perceived by the student.

A related example may be taken from the case of the student's own artistic development. If a beginner is asked too early in his training to reproduce faithfully all the detail of a complicated subject, then he cannot *gradually* develop skill. Worse, he may be put off by failure. If the instructor demands imitation by the beginner of a technique that is too advanced, then, again, a *gradation* of development is hindered, if not actually prevented.

**Figure 3.8.** Vincent Van Gogh. *The Starry Night.* 1889. Oil on canvas. 29 x 36¼". Collection, The Museum of Modern Art, New York. Acquired through the Lillie P. Bliss Bequest.

Discussion on this term should suggest the use of many appropriate examples. A piece of music that has a climax, a race that is won by a tremendous effort in the concluding distance, or a ball game—all may furnish appropriate referents. This latter example may be particularly appropriate. Not all games have their high point in the concluding minutes, some being decided at an earlier climactic moment. The parallels in art can be presented more easily if such commonplace examples, drawn from the students' everyday experiences, are used.

## A Syllabus for Understanding of Design— Grades One Through Six

### What Design Means

#### Grade 1

*Behavioral Objective.* To encourage the students to notice the use of rhythmic elements within a composition.

*Presentation.* Show the class some reproductions and examples in which the artist has used rhythm. These examples should be placed on view for some days prior to the discussion. Examples of this rhythm in terms of painting might be Piet Mondrian's *Broadway Boogie-Woogie* (1945). Another example of rhythm in a three-dimensional work might be seen in an African sculpture, such as a Dogon ancestor figure.

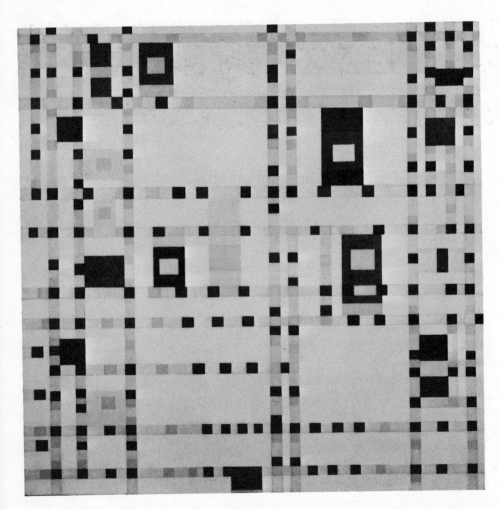

**Figure 3.9.**   Piet Mondrian. *Broadway Boogie-Woogie.* 1942-43. Oil on canvas. 50 x 50 inches. Collection, The Museum of Modern Art, New York.

*Discussion.* The following questions might be used as a starting point for class discussion.

Is there a rhythm in this work?
How do these repeating lines, shapes, etc., help you understand the total work?
Do these rhythms occur enough times to make a sequence?

*Summation.* The development in the students of an ability to see and use the rhythm of repeated shapes, motifs, etc., in their own work.

### Grade 2

*Behavioral Objective.* To make the students aware of the various methods used by an artist to create balance. To help them appreciate the ways in which mass or "weight" can balance forms of differing size.

*Presentation.* For several days prior to the discussion, exhibit some reproductions of typically symmetric and asymmetric arrangements. One obvious one is a photograph of the Parthenon. The value of this can be more adequately perceived if close-up photographs showing the "entasis" (or swelling out) of the pillars are available. Other examples of balance might be the sculpture (recently damaged) Michelangelo's *Pieta* or Polliauolo's *Hercules and Antaeus*. Another example might be a mobile of Alexander Calder, or the *Cubi* series of David Smith. In painting, such examples as Pablo Picasso's *Three Musicians* might be selected.

**Figure 3.10.** Model of the Parthenon in Athens. Greek Architecture. V Century B.C. The Metropolitan Museum of Art. Purchase, 1890, Levi Hale Willard Bequest.

**Figure 3.11.** Antonio Polliauolo. *Hercules and Antaeus*. Museo Nazionale del Bargello, Florence. SCALA–New York/Florence.

**Figure 3.12.**

*Above:* David Smith. *Cubi XVII.* 1963. Dallas Museum of Fine Arts. The Eugene and Margaret McDermott Fund.

*Left:* David Smith. *Cubi XVIII.* Courtesy, Museum of Fine Arts, Boston. Gift of Stephen D. Paine.

*Discussion.* Discuss the forces, or reactions, which make for *balance* of differing forms. Discuss symmetry and asymmetry. The following questions might provide starting points:

Does color help create balance?
Does the shape become important in this respect?
How do relative sizes of things in a work of art affect balance?
Can there be successful balance between very large and very small forms?

*Summation.* A good activity in the studio work of the class following this discussion might be for them to work first on the making of mobiles. However, they should not merely stop at this. It might be well, after they have made their mobiles, if the class were to make paintings or two-dimensional drawings from the perceived arrangement of the moving forms within the mobile. Moreover, the mobile forms themselves must be kept relatively simple so that the drawing from them need not be too difficult for attainment by these students.

Figure 3.13.    Pablo Picasso. *Three Musicians.* 1921 (summer). Oil on canvas. 6'7" x 7' 3¾". Collection, The Museum of Modern Art, New York. Mrs. Simon Guggenheim Fund.

### Grade 3

*Behavioral Objective.* To increase the students' awareness of proportion as a means of achieving a good design.

*Presentation.* Exhibit the drawings of da Vinci's *Vitruvian Man.* Other examples might be the ballet dancers of Edgar Degas. Similarly, Modigliani's *Head of a Girl* might be an example of balance. In three-dimensional work, a sculpture of Rodin, preferably a well-known one such as *The Thinker,* might be suitable. Other examples might be from less obvious works. For example, one of Utrillo's street scenes might also be appropriate. Encourage the students, when looking at these prior to discussion, to look at the proportions and arrangements within the works.

**Figure 3.14.** Auguste Rodin, 1840-1917. *The Thinker.* The Metropolitan Museum of Art. Gift of Thomas F. Ryan, 1910.

*Discussion.* Questions to be asked at this time might be similar to those below:

How can the artist be sure of correct proportion?
Discuss the various ways of making *measurement.*
Is there any rule for correct proportion?
How about cartoons and caricatures—don't they break the rules?
Why do we need proportion?
When can we ignore it?

*Summation.* Have the students make clay models, working from a friend or another student who is posing as a model. Perhaps they might make face-to-face portraits, working from one to another. Alternatively, self-portraits may be made by using mirrors. During the time that the students are engaged in their art activity, have them be aware of the uses of measurement in order to obtain correct proportion where they feel it is necessary to obtain a satisfactory and pleasing result. Do not, however, overstress the need for rigid measurement.

## Grade 4

*Behavioral Objective.* To have the students aware of the importance of gradation. To encourage them to realize the artist's arrangement, which by the use of certain elements within the total work creates a climax.

*Presentation.* Choose certain reproductions and display them with a note to look for the arrangements that encourage the viewer to seek further within the work. One example which might be used would be a reproduction of the painting *The Scream* by Edvard Munch.

*Discussion.* Use the discussion time for examining the reasons why the paintings that you have displayed can work successfully and stand alone on their merits. Questions that might be used to stimulate discussion should be as follows:

Is there a rhythm in this painting?
What of the overall design?
Why has this been successful in creating a gradation?
What variations can easily be seen in the work?

*Summation.* If the student can apply, or tries to apply, any of the forms of design that we have seen represented, this should be encouraged.

## Grade 5

*Behavioral Objective.* To encourage student awareness of the ways in which design elements may be used together in a work of art.

*Presentation.* Display some of the works already seen in this series to illustrate rhythm, balance, proportion, gradation, and add some new works to illustrate all aspects of these.

*Discussion.* The discussion should relate back to other topics already discussed in the series and should also develop new insights. Questions that might be asked would be the following:

How well did the artist arrange the parts of the picture?
What shapes or areas in it seem to be related to each other?
Are there lines, dots, etc., which seem to repeat a pattern?
Are there lines or shapes that seem to be parallel?

**Figure 3.15.** Edvard Munch. *The Scream*. 1893. Reproduced by courtesy of the National Gallery, Oslo, Norway.

*Summation.* At this stage, students should be given a more formal exercise in their activity. They might be given a choice of elements from which to "compose" an art work, for example, a geometric shape superimposed upon a free form.

### Grade 6

*Behavioral Objective.* To discuss the effect of an artist's design upon the composition. To show certain examples to the students which will indicate means and methods used by the artist in his task of visual arrangement.

*Presentation.* As preparation, give a brief lecture in which you will show examples of famous artists who are using or have worked with design elements that the children may begin to use in their own work. Have the students bring in pictures from magazines showing the same situations.

*Discussion.* Questions should be asked to motivate the students to use for their own work what they see in these works.

How can you use and obtain the same feeling of dimension in your work?
Is there a design quality to this painting?
Does the artist cover the page?
Does the artist divide his paper or canvas into areas?

*Summation.* Encourage the students to bring in items that correlate with the discussion. Have the students recognize the different techniques and attempt to use them in their own work. Stress the definition of *design* in the classic sense of composition.

# a further step 4
## toward appreciation

**The Art Subject Areas**

It should be explained to the students that just as there are many different subjects they learn about in school, so there are areas or different techniques and mediums in art. In the mass of school subjects that we call the curriculum, there are subjects that are practical and technical. There are also subjects that are academic or have to do with the reading of material in books or the obtaining of information from films, transparencies, or other means. The art curriculum, therefore, includes the same types of groupings. In the case of art, however, they refer to the learning about, the talking about and criticizing of, and the creating of works of art. Having drawn these parallels in order that the students may be able to understand the art areas, we can then proceed to present them sequentially, as follows below.

## *Drawing*

### PENCIL

Most of us were accustomed to drawing with a pencil early in our lives. There are various degrees of graphite included in a pencil, and these vary from soft to hard quality. The soft lead pencil gives a thick, black line, characterized by a soft quality. The hard lead pencil, on the other hand, gives a thin, light line which has extreme precision but does not have great textural quality.

### CRAYONS

Crayons are another type of drawing medium with which we have had experience from quite an early age. Crayons are wax sticks of color and, because of the wax contained within them, produce a hard, shiny application. This application of the color on paper or similar surfaces does not need "fixing" with any kind of sprayed-on gum or varnish. The fixing process is usually done with media that are liable to smudge. Wax crayons are notable for their ease in usage, their extreme practicality in that they are nontoxic, and for the fact that the range of colors is varied and brilliant.

## CHALKS

Chalks are of various types, but they are made from dry pigments in powder form. These powdered colors are of fair and good qualities. Both of them need a fixing process to avoid being smudged after they are applied. The commonest types of chalks are the same as those used for the old-fashioned slate or blackboard colors. These have a somewhat coarse texture and are limited in scope and practicality. However, one has only to see the work of a "pavement artist" in a large city (such as London, England) to realize that like any other medium in skilled hands, they can produce a virtuoso performance.

The other types of chalks are known as pastels. These are also powder colors, but they are of better quality in that the powder is ground to a much finer consistency. Pastels have great range and brilliancy and when properly used develop a quality known as *bloom*. This bloom very soon loses its lustrous quality if the work is not fixed soon after the color is applied.

All kinds of chalks can be applied to various surfaces other than paper. For example, they may be applied to wall areas (as in a mural). They may also be applied to other mediums, such as the lithographer's stone or plate.

## INK

Ink drawing may be made using pens or points of straws or reeds, with various commercially produced items such as felt-tip pens or ball-points. The most classical kind of drawing is that done with the pen or point. In the case of the pen, it is often made of a flexible metal such as steel which, being divided by a cut in the center, allows the point to spread out, creating a thick or thin line. The great flexibility allows the artist to create widely differing linear qualities. Drawing with straws, reeds, or sticks produces varying types of lines. If the straws are used as is, the textural quality can sometimes be very pleasing. In this sense, some Oriental examples may profitably be shown to students to illustrate this type of work, such as *Bamboo* attributed to Wu-Chen.

More modern commercial production processes have produced new drawing instruments. Of these the first was the ball-point, and in spite of the somewhat "hard" quality of this instrument, in the hands of a skilled practitioner some good textural imagery can be produced. The felt-tip, on the other hand, produces bold, black linear statements. With large-scale drawings, the felt-tip can be used to produce an additional textural element, which, on such a scale, can give a piece of work great strength.

## CHARCOAL

There are various degrees of charcoal, giving a range from hard to soft. With charcoal the end of the stick may be used to make lines; alternatively it can be held sideways and can be used to make large areas of texture. There are also uses in terms of rubbing or smudging the applied black. Some academic uses of the medium have included white card points which are used to heighten the effects of value by providing white areas within originally created black ones. These white card tips produce areas with great precision. The disadvantage of charcoal, like that of chalk and pastels, is that once again the work requires a fixative spray in order to avoid inadvertent smudging when the design is completed. Charcoal can also be used as a preliminary for painting on canvas. The charcoal stick readily makes a mark on a canvas which remains with some persistence until covered by paint.

**Figure 4.1.** Attributed to Wu-Chen. *Bamboo*. Reproduced by permission of the Trustees of the British Museum.

BRUSH DRAWING

This kind of drawing can be made in ink or in watercolor. Sometimes watercolor or ink may be combined with pen drawing. This is usually referred to as *pen and wash*. As an alternative, the ink or watercolor areas may be heightened with a pencil line application. This is known as *pencil and wash*. Alternatively, brush drawing may be done, as in the academic sense of watercolor, by the application of washes. Another use for brush drawing is with the so-called *dry-brush* technique. Usually with dry-brush drawing only one color is used. The effects produce high textural qualities and a grayness which is obtained by the paper shining through the color.

*Painting*

### WATERCOLOR

Watercolor is also sometimes referred to as *aquarelle*. When this term is used, it applies to *transparent* watercolor. There are several different techniques for the application of transparent watercolor. However, the most commonly used and the classically academic use of the medium is by the application of washes. A *wash* is a small quantity of color mixed with an amount of water so as to produce a transparent area of color through which the underlying color of the paper will show. These washes are usually quick in drying, and they produce the sparkling transparencies which are the hallmark of the academic watercolor technique. The makers of paper have for many years produced special high-quality *hot press* paper which allows for a whiteness level to create the kind of sparkle that is so typical of transparent watercolor. There are, however, other things to try in watercolor, for example, the pigments such as gouache or tempera.

### GOUACHE

*Gouache* is a French word used for "opaque." It is a nontransparent watercolor pigment. It is mixed with a white ingredient in order to produce the opaque quality for which it is noted. All the colors available, therefore, are somewhat "flat" because of the white ingredient.

### TEMPERA

*Tempera*, in a manner similar to gouache, is an opaque color. In this case, however, the pigment is mixed with oil and watercolor. Tempera paints, therefore, produce colors somewhat more brilliant than the nontransparent watercolors. They are often used for school art classes.

### CASEIN

These paints have a glue binding agent. They are mixed with water thinners and dry in a matte surface. They are also extremely quick to dry. However, the disadvantage of them is that they cannot be applied very thickly; they are very brittle and therefore "crack off" easily on paper or canvas. They are also resistant to mixing with other paints that are not compatible with them.

### OIL PAINTING

Oil painting developed from the need for the Medieval and Early Renaissance painters to develop a paint medium that was resistant to dampness. Various claims are made for the discovery, some attributable to the Venetians who found the damp climate of the Adriatic city played havoc with their panel paintings. Other attributes are given to the Northern Renaissance painters in the Low Countries.

The qualities of oil paintings are fairly well known. They are, of course, extremely long-lasting. They can be cleaned (albeit with great care), and they have a range of brilliant colors. They must be applied to a surface which has previously been prepared with an oil primer. This ground, usually white, is suitable for the "squaring" technique or for drawing in charcoal by the painter. There are many, many technical applications of the oil painting medium. These range from *glazing* to heavy impasto. In the former, a thin film of color diluted with a thinning agent such as linseed oil is used to produce a transparent effect. In the latter, the paint is applied very thickly to provide a raised, textured surface to the painting. Glazed applications are often applied over another color, thus giving a warm glow which is in some respects similar to the effect of watercolor. The impasto technique often shows the brushstrokes or marks of the palette knife used to apply the thick masses of paint.

### FRESCO

Fresco is the art of painting on a plaster surface, such as a wall. It comes from an Italian word meaning "fresh." However, the term *wall-painting* does not always imply the use of fresco. Fresco was used in Italy from the thirteenth to the sixteenth centuries, and perhaps in Mexico by Diego Rivera. There are two types of fresco practiced. One is called *fresco secco* which is painted on dry plaster. It has one major defect, namely, the paint tends to flake off with age, as with many interior walls which have a distemper-type pigment application. True fresco, or *buon fresco,* is the most permanent form of wall decoration. This pigment is applied to a wet plaster. Because of this, a chemical reaction takes place between

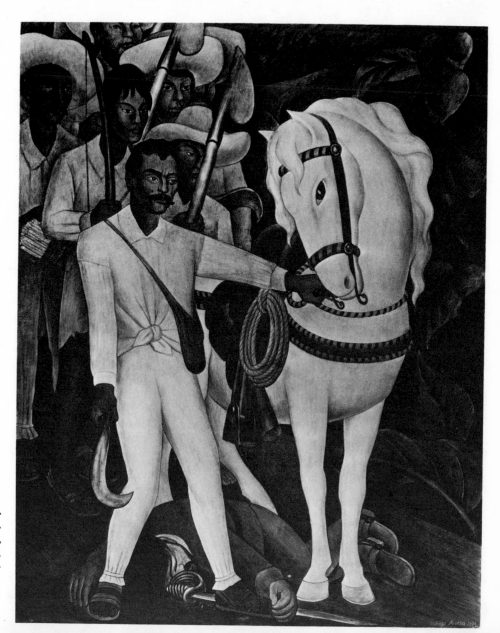

**Figure 4.2.** Diego Rivera. *Agrarian Leader Zapata.* 1931. Fresco. 93¾ x 74″. Collection, The Museum of Modern Art, New York. Abby Aldrich Rockefeller Fund.

the colors and the wet plaster, and this means that the colors become part of the wall itself. For this reason, the color seldom, if ever, deteriorates. So long-lasting is it that in some buildings which have had to be demolished, a complete fresco wall decoration has been removed intact by the use of special techniques.

There are other types of wall-painting known as murals, but these are not the same as fresco. In the case of the mural, it is often an application of tempera or similar pigments to a wall surface. Many of these were seen in the WPA art programs in this country during the late 1930s and early 1940s.

**Figure 4.6.** George Biddle. *Sweatshop*. Study for fresco in fifth-floor stairwell—Justice Department Building, Washington, D.C. c. 1935. Section of Painting and Sculpture. Tempera on Masonite. 4¾ x 31⅝. Collection, University of Maryland.

## ENCAUSTIC

Encaustic painting is done by the use of wax colors which are applied to a heat-resistant surface. This heat-resistant surface, such as a metal sheet or tile, is then placed in a small kiln, or oven, to enable heat to bake or burn the colors into the surface.

An elaboration of this technique is seen in the art of Cloisonné. The artist creates a design by using lines made with little "walls" of silver. In between these silver walls, he pours different-colored encaustic paints. The whole is then fired in a kiln. Very delightful jewel-like effects are obtained from this demanding technique.

### Stained Glass

This classical technique is principally known for its application to the decoration of religious buildings. It has been used in more modern times, however, for the decoration of secular buildings. The technique is to color pieces of glass which are then joined by strips of lead. These designs, when viewed from a distance, have a tremendous jewel-like quality. However, when one moves more closely toward them, the dark lines of the lead strips act in a somewhat divisive fashion upon the total design. An additional complication is for the stained-glass artist to further paint on additional colors, which are then baked onto the glass by firing in a kiln.

### Printmaking

The art of printmaking, or graphics as it is sometimes called, is that of producing many copies of one design or picture. It is thus a reproductive technique which produces "multiple originals." All prints are obtained by pressing together the paper and a printing surface. The printing surface has usually received an application of ink or similar pigment. There are various types of printmaking.

## RELIEF PRINTING

These types of prints are made by cutting away the negative areas. The areas left "in relief," that is, raised up, accept the ink, or pigment; the cut-away areas do not. This results in the raised area producing the positive image and the lowered area producing the negative spaces around it. This technique is most often seen in the linocut or the woodcut.

## INTAGLIO

In this process the reverse from the relief prints is true. Here, those parts which are lowered carry ink which is held within them. When the paper is pressed together with this surface, the ink is squeezed out from them on to the paper. The intaglio lines are scratched, cut, or etched with acid. These types of prints allow great precision in line, together with a wide variety of textural effects.

## LITHOGRAPHY

A design is drawn with a greasy pencil or a wax crayon upon a stone or a zinc plate. The particular stone used is an extremely densely-packed limestone which usually comes from an area in Bavaria, Germany. The stone or zinc plate is then wetted, and when ink is applied the ink will not mix with the water. However, the water does not "take" upon the greasy lines of the crayon. The ink can therefore interact and fix upon these lines. When the paper is pressed to them, the negative areas (which are wet) do not reproduce any image. The positive areas which have the ink on top of the greasy line produce an image.

### SERIGRAPHY

This is also referred to as silk-screen printing. In this technique, a stencil is used to allow the pressing of color through the cutouts. This makes a printed design of formal geometric quality upon the paper sheet. Each time that the screen is raised, a fresh sheet is inserted below it. The screen is then once again applied with paint which, when squeezed through the cutouts, produces a print.

### COMMERCIAL PRINTS OR REPRODUCTIONS

Most recently there has been somewhat of a storm in the art world over the tremendous increase in commercially produced prints which are sold as "originals" or "limited editions." There is considerable controversy over such questions as the artistic integrity of turning over a plate to a commercial printer for reproduction; whether an offset image put on paper by photographic means can be called original; and what the limits are for a "limited edition." Some opinion holds that the print should be inked and put through a press one at a time by hand. Others would call the new offset images "original" prints. The dilemma is as yet unresolved.

The more commonly known "prints" are, in fact, reproductions. At one time, most art history instructors used these for study. Now color slides have replaced them. Many printed reproductions are offered to the general public, however, and their cheapness is often the principal reason for their popularity.

## Sculpture

Sculpture takes two forms: one is relief, the other is free-standing. There are two types of relief: high and low. In both cases the sculpture is not totally three-dimensional but stands out from a flat surface area. If the figures, objects, or forms of the work project only slightly from the plane surface, it is known as *low relief*. Where the objects or forms have a *high relief*, they stand out so much from the plane surface that they are almost freed from it.

Free-standing or three-dimensional sculpture is the more typical form that we see, for example, in the statue.

### MODELING

Modeling can be made in clay or wax. Sometimes an armature is used to hold up the form. This is necessary where the form is larger at the top than at the bottom and might therefore collapse upon itself without some support. If the model is to be baked or fired in a kiln, it is often hollow. This process is effected by the cutting in half of the clay or wax model which is then hollowed out, and the two halves are rejoined.

### CASTING

In casting, a plaster mold, or sometimes a sand mold, is placed around the model. The model may be of clay or some other material, such as wax. With plaster casting, the mold is pulled away in sections. These sections are then put together again to be filled with new plaster. An alternative method is the *lost wax* technique. Here the wax is heated after the mold has been put around it. The wax melts and runs out of the mold, leaving it free to accept the new casting. Sand-molding is used to cast molten metal.

### CARVING

Carving is a subtractive sculptural process where the material is taken away from its original source. Carving can be made in wood, stone, or more exotic materials. The carver needs great care, for he must also think about what he is going to make before he begins. The African carver usually works from one block.

**Figure 4.7.** Dogon. *Ancestor Figure Sitting on Stool.* Reproduced by courtesy of the University of Pennsylvania, Philadelphia.

**CONSTRUCTION**

Here the sculptor builds the art form by joining pieces together. Sometimes metal pieces are joined by soldering or welding. Wood is also used; and in more recent times, much plastic and other synthetic materials are used.

**Figure 4.8.** Naum Gabo. *Column.* 1923. Plastic, wood, metal. 41½″ high. The Solomon R. Guggenheim Museum.

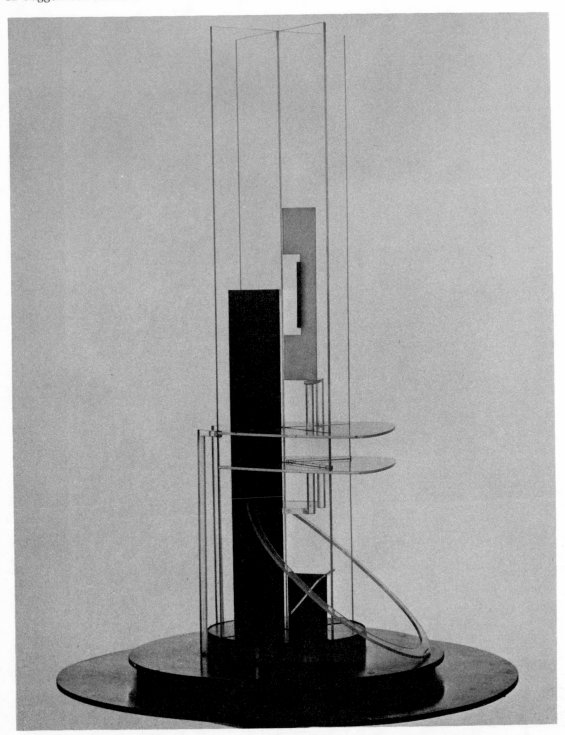

### KINETIC, OR MOVING, SCULPTURE

Here the form is moved by either natural or man-made power sources. In the case of the mobile, the source is often only the natural one of currents of air. Man-made power sources are usually small electric motors. Some more recent kinetic sculpture has taken an additional dimension in the use of light (neon tube), and even musical accompaniment.

**Figure 4.9.** L. Moholy-Nagy. *Light-Space Modulator.* Sculpture. Reproduced by courtesy of Busch-Reisinger Museum, Harvard University, Cambridge, Massachusetts.

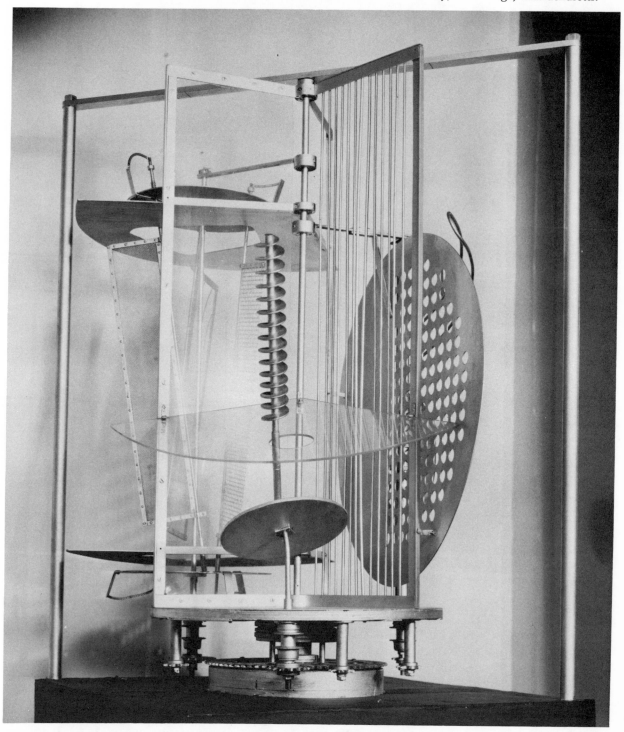

## Photography

Photography has two forms—still photography and cinematography, or movies. The artist-photographer uses the effects of light falling upon sensitized film. In order to do this, he needs a tool. This tool is the camera. By increasing the amount of time when the light is touching the film or by widening the aperture to permit greater amounts of light to touch the film, the artist can create different effects.

**Figure 4.10.** Richard Lippold. *Variation within a Sphere, No. 10; The Sun*. The Metropolitan Museum of Art, Fletcher Fund, 1956.

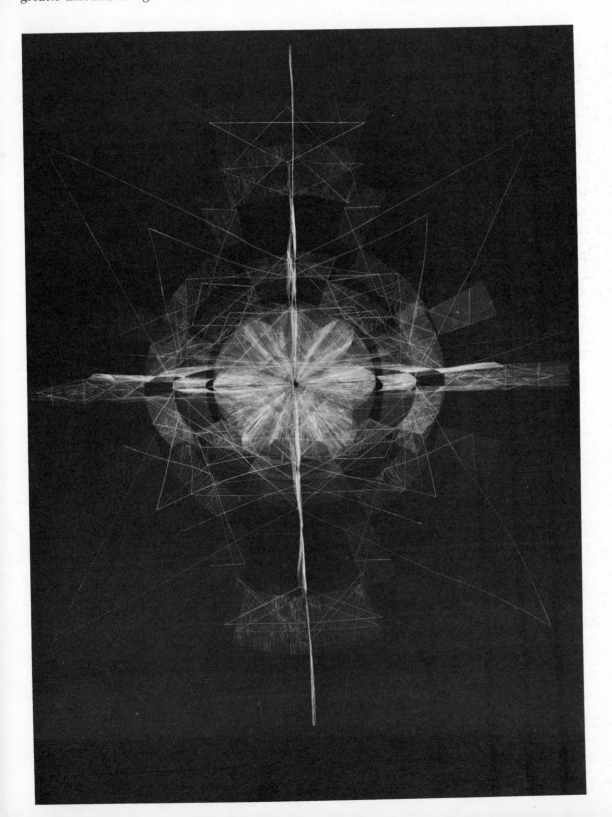

Different types of light emanate from the sun, from artificial light such as a lamp or bulb, and from moonlight. The artist-photographer can use hard, bright light to make a clear, sharp picture, or he can use soft, "cloudy" daylight for a more romantic or mysterious image. He can direct light to bring out the form or to make it look more solid. He may use reflected light, or even shadows and reflections, to make a better photograph.

In the making of movies, all the above light sources are used, together with the ability to *pan*. This is the ability to move the *eye* of the camera across a whole scene. Another invention, the *zoom* lens enables the camera to see an object or scene in close-up, and then, equally easily, to move out again to a long-distance view of these same things.

## Activities to Emphasize the Differing Kinds of Art Imagery—Grades One Through Six

### The Art Subject Areas

#### Grade 1

*Behavioral Objectives.* To enable the students to examine and to become aware of the special qualities inherent in drawing with various media.

*Presentation.* Use some film loops or movie films on the subject of drawing. Take as a theme in drawing the subject of animals. Put on display such works as the drawing *A Hare* by Albrecht Dürer. Alternatively or additiona'ly, display the *Monkeys* by Pisanello. Other examples might be taken from Chinese brush painting, or modern works in pastel, charcoal, etc.

**Figure 4.11.** Pisanello. *Leaves from a Sketchbook: Monkeys.* The Louvre, Paris. Réunion des Musées Nationaux.

*Discussion.* Having allowed the students to examine the examples and having presented them with some visual examples of drawing, develop discussion through the following types of questions:

How has Pisanello used his drawing ability to capture the feeling of movement?
How does Dürer use many lines (or a texture) to portray the coat of the hare?

*Summation.* The class can experiment with a "sampler" of different drawing marks and techniques. Later, these can be applied in series from pencil, through crayon, to brush.

## Grade 2

*Behavioral Objective.* To examine the various techniques of painting so as to be able to recognize some and possibly to experiment with them in one's own work.

*Presentation.* Display some reproductions of work in various media. These should include works in aquarelle (watercolor), opaque watercolor, tempera color, oil color, and even, possibly, some stained glass. The problem of providing examples of this work might possibly be solved if the work could be borrowed from a local community college art department, a four-year college art department, an art school, or possibly a local art guild. The examples should be from the institution's students' work, if possible.

*Discussion.* For this discussion it would be advantageous to have a member of the institution from which the work has been borrowed (such as a faculty member or student) visit and lead the discussion. Some of the questions that he might ask the students could take the following forms:

Why does a transparent watercolor seem to possess a glowing quality?
What can we note when viewing impasto oil color?
How does an artist work with stained glass?

*Summation.* It might be proper to encourage the students to experiment using colored plastic so as to create designs similar to those of stained glass. These designs can be hung against a windowpane to obtain the proper effect.

Another experimentation with the students could be to attempt to use some of the elementary techniques of watercolor and oil color. However, the art of watercolor is an extremely delicate procedure, and grade-two students will find it difficult. Similarly, oil color, because of its impracticality in usage in a non-art environment, might not be a suitable medium for this age group. Thickly mixed powder colors can be used to create impasto effects, and this might be a substitution for oils. It is important that the student work in this regard should go only so far in technique as the students' readiness level would indicate.

## Grade 3

*Behavioral Objective.* To encourage the student to appreciate the qualities of a "multiple original." To give some knowledge of the print media and the method of reproduction.

*Presentation.* Display a series of prints, using, if possible, the following media:

| | | |
|---|---|---|
| Wood block | Engraving | Lithograph |
| Wood engraving | Silk screen, or serigraph | Etching |

As with grade two, try to obtain examples from a college or similar art department.

*Discussion.* Again, as with the previous year, it would be advantageous to have someone from the contributing institution visit the class and lead a discussion on the examples that have been displayed. Ideally, also, it would be very advantageous for the students to view at one and the same time both the block from which the image was printed and the print which has been made. A short description by a student or faculty member of the technical process involved would also be of great value and would arouse considerable interest.

*Summation.* Having established in the students' ideas the scope and advantages of the print media, allow them to develop their own work with simple forms of it. Examples might be carried out in linoleum block, tin-can etchings, etc. There is also a considerable range of cheaply produced printing materials for this kind of work.

## Grade 4

*Behavioral Objective.* To encourage the students to become knowledgeable on some methods of producing sculpture.

*Presentation.* Show examples of simple *additive* sculpture. These might be prehistoric or "primitive" clay figures. Also show further examples of *subtractive* sculpture. These might take the form of African, Polynesian, or similar wood carving. Other examples should be shown of sculpture in stone (for example, Verrochio's *David*) or plaster casts or bronze figures (for example, Degas' *Ballet Girl*).

*Below:*

**Figure 4.12.** Andrea del Verrocchio. *David.* Museo del Bargello, Florence. SCALA—New York/Florence.

*Below right:*

**Figure 4.13.** Edgar Hilaire Germain Degas. *Ballet Girl.* The Metropolitan Museum of Art. Bequest of Mrs. H. O. Havemeyer, 1929. The H. O. Havemeyer Collection.

*Discussion.* The questions might take the following forms:

How has the addition of parts helped to complete the figure?
How cleverly has the sculptor cut away parts so as to leave the form standing free?
What must a sculptor be careful of when he makes a mold to cast a form?

*Summation.* Allow the class to make clay forms and to make simple plaster casts from them. These would probably be best begun with relief sculpture rather than with sculpture in the round.

## Grade 5

*Behavioral Objective.* To show the students the important qualities of a major art form—the photograph. It is hoped to inculcate the realization of the differences between the artist-photographer and the mere taker of snapshots.

*Presentation.* Display early examples of the daguerreotype portrait, the work of Matthew Brady (in his recording of the Civil War), early still photography such as the *views of the Cincinnati waterfront*, pages 78-79, and more recent work of such people as Jerry Uelsmann.

*Discussion.* Questions following upon some days of examination of displayed examples might take the following forms:

What is the most important element in a photograph?
How does the artist use it in this example?
Is it possible to "compose" a picture in a camera viewfinder before pressing the shutter?

*Summation.* Allow the students to take photographs and have the results processed commercially at a bulk rate. This should not preclude anyone's participating, since the costs are relatively low.

## Grade 6

*Behavioral Objective.* To bring to the students an awareness of some of the essential qualities of movie-making. To experiment on their own account.

*Presentation.* Show carefully selected movies to demonstrate the art of animation, etc. Some early examples of *Felix the Cat* together with some Walt Disney examples would be an ideal presentation.

*Discussion.* Encourage the students to comment while the films are being shown and then develop questions as follows:

Does this film seem to lead the viewer's eye?
Does the rhythmic repetition amuse us or even make us laugh aloud?

*Summation.* At this point we might try some student work direct on movie film. Film leader (white coating) is obtainable from any laboratory which processes movie film, often at no charge. The film leader should be placed on top of long strips of white paper and taped along the length of a series of tables. Allow the students to sit on either side, armed with paintbrushes and various colors. Have them paint directly onto the film and in some cases scratch through the film leader with sharp instruments. Do not, however, allow the film to be punctured. After a certain amount of drawing and decoration has been placed on the film, it can then be run through a movie projector, and the class can see immediately the results of their own "animations." After one such work session, the enthusiasm will often generate quite inventive developments. With older students it is possible to tape sound onto movie film and to create some interesting blendings of music and animated artistic forms. The work of the Canadian film maker Norman McLaren can be obtained from the Canadian Consulate in Chicago. Examples of such films might be *Serenal, Short and Suite,* or *A Phantasy.*

**Figure 4.14.** Matthew Brady. *The "Keystone" Battery of Pennsylvania.* Reproduced by courtesy of the Brady-Handy Collection, Library of Congress, Washington, D.C.

**Figure 4.15.** William Southgate Porter and Charles Fontayne. *View of Cincinnati Waterfront 1848* (5 photographs). Photographs courtesy of The Public Library of Cincinnati and Hamilton County. Reproduced by permission.

# 5 criticism must be based on "know-how"

## Ways in Which the Artist Works

It is important to examine the various ways in which the artist worked in the past and the ways in which the artist works in modern times. These topics, to some extent, will overlap with the already developed series on the elements of art and the functions of design. However, we can tentatively examine with students of elementary age some of the *isms* and, most certainly, some of the *schools* that have flourished during the history of art. It might be well to begin by having a series of discussions on the development of the art school in Medieval and Renaissance Italy. The art centers in Renaissance Italy are usually considered to be those of Florence, Siena, Pisa, Bologna, Rome, Parma, Padua, and Venice. We could develop an understanding of the idea of the school by showing, in series, displays of reproductions from each of these centers.

An alternative method might be to discuss the work of Northern Europe and the various masters who flourished, particularly in the Low Countries. The theme of the monastic artists might be developed, showing how the monk in his cell often produced beautifully illustrated books and that these are works of art in their own right. All this introductory material will help prepare the students to reexamine both technique and composition in order to establish the various ways in which an artist may express his ideas.

## *Drawing, or Graphic Expression*

In traditional artistic practice there is little or no free rein given to emotion, or feeling. There would be, usually, the artistic commitment to the representation of natural forms of things. There would be a struggle to express in art terms a perceived object. Sometimes the artist is exploring new principles of drawing, as, for example, the drawing of a crosier, or bishop's crook, by Martin Schöngauer, made in the 1400s; the design for a chalice (1400s) by Paolo Uccello; and the sketches of Leonardo da Vinci. Sometimes there is a commitment to human form, as with Michelangelo's drawings, or an even deeper commitment to self-analysis, as in the self-portraits of Dürer and Rembrandt (and Graham Sutherland in this century). This is in direct contrast to more recent work in abstraction. Here the artist

*Page 81:*

**Figure 5.1.** Antonello da Messina. *St. Jerome in His Study.* Reproduced by courtesy of the Trustees, The National Gallery, London.

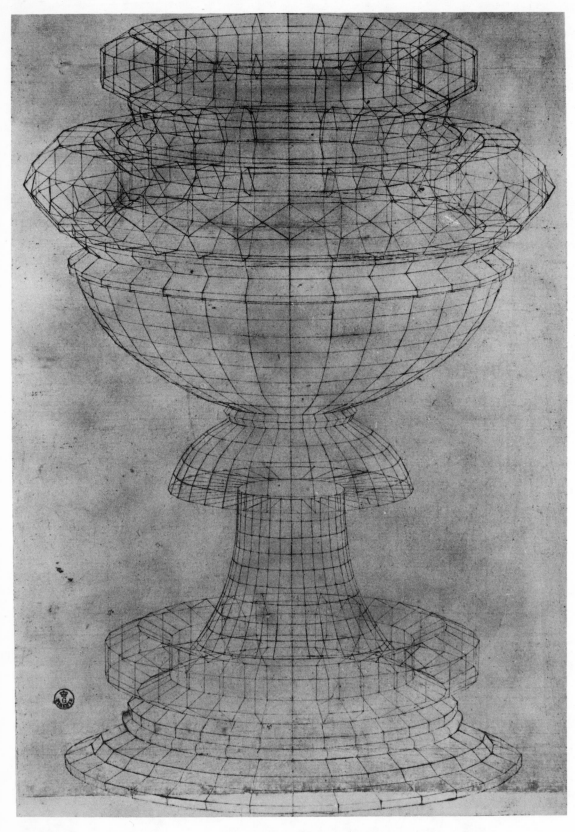

**Figure 5.2.**    Paolo Uccello. *Faceted Chalice.* Uffizi, Florence. SCALA—New York/Florence.

**Figure 5.3.** Albrecht Dürer. *Self Portrait*. Alte Pinakothek, Munich. SCALA—New York/Florence.

**Figure 5.4.** Rembrandt. *Self-Portrait*. Reproduced by courtesy of The Greater London Council as Trustees of the Iveagh Bequest, Kenwood.

exposes his personal feelings through his method of expression. We might use as such examples the drawings of Paul Klee, Piet Mondrian, and Jackson Pollock.

Not all contemporary drawings are pure abstraction, however. Picasso's drawings of beasts (*Minotauromachy*), the humanistic drawings of Giacometti, and Bernard Buffet's schematic precision are each examples of twentieth-century draftsmanship.

**Figure 5.5.** Pablo Picasso. *Minotauromachy.* 1935. Etching, printed in black. 22¼″ x 29¼″. Collection, The Museum of Modern Art, New York.

#### A NOTE ON COMPOSITION

In the traditional practice of art, the composition is a deliberate arrangement of elements within the work. There is a distinct attempt, consciously made by the artist, to create a formal design from these elements. Thus we see from the earliest times, through Medieval, Renaissance, and up to very recent times, this formal engagement with the arranged shapes and forms. As examples of this, we might use Egyptian paintings, some formal geometrically arranged paintings from the Renaissance, and the work of the French Academicians of the early nineteenth century.

## Abstract Composition

In contrast are the more recent developments in abstraction, where the elements of the art work are often cast aside in favor of a neoformalism with a universal application. An example of this is Mark Tobey's *Edge of August, 1953.* To further develop the theme of abstraction in painting, we might examine the development of the work of Piet Mondrian. For example, his *Still Life with Ginger Pot I,* which is in a museum in The Hague, was painted in 1911. A similar development in the same year and given the same title shows considerable variations of the elements in a formalistic fashion.

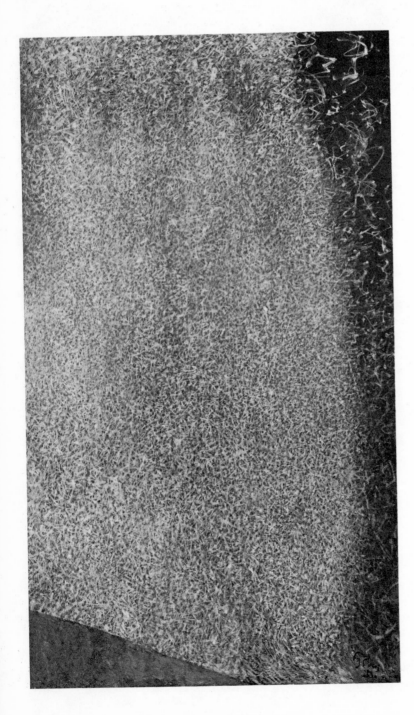

*Left:*
**Figure 5.6.**    Mark Tobey. *Edge of August.* 1953. Casein on composition board. 48″ x 28″. Collection, The Museum of Modern Art, New York.

*Page 87:*
**Figure 5.7.**    Piet Mondrian. *(top) Still-life with Ginger Pot I.* 1911.
*(bottom) Still-life with Ginger Pot II.* 1911. Collection of Gemeentemuseum, The Hague. Reproduced by permission.

In what Lucie-Smith terms *Late Modern* we can trace compositional "modes" through the abstract Expressionism of the 1940s and 1950s (Helen Frankenthaler, Arshile Gorky, Philip Guston, Willem de Kooning, etc. ) to the emerging redefinitions of Hans Hofman, Jasper Johns, and Franz Kline, which lead us to the 1960s' Pop scene (Roy Lichtenstein, Robert Rauschenberg, and Andy Warhol). Most recently we have seen the Op (optical) artists' commitment to retinal assault (Richard Anuskiewicz, Larry Poons, Bridget Riley, Victor Vasarely, etc.).

To attempt to discuss, here, in historical (or cultural, or any other developmental) sequence the totality of the artistic mode is impossible. For the guidance of the teacher planning such topical analyses, what follows is a series of outlines of *some* major areas, with emphasis on the more recent developments. These latter are often the topics that the layman finds most difficult to comprehend.

### Genre Painting

A French word is used to describe the painting of scenes from everyday life. This word is *genre*. Many of these paintings show scenes in everyday life either of commonplace "folksy" activities or of interiors of homes with the life going on inside them. Genre pictures were painted for ordinary people and no special thought was needed for the viewer to understand the meaning. Genre painting seems to have flourished most in Holland during the seventeenth century. This type of painting came about largely because of the reversion from religious painting at this time; also because the Dutch paintings were not too large to hang comfortably in a small private home, as opposed to the large religious works which could only be hung in great public buildings.

Examples of the work of the Dutch genre painters might be from Jan Steen, Vermeer, and, notably, Pieter de Hooch, whose courtyard scenes are of great interest as an example of the life of the time. Other genre paintings were by Chardin, a French artist, and by Murillo in Spain. In England the greatest genre painter was William Hogarth. He painted scenes which the general public did not usually visualize. His pictures show a riotous and sometimes evil society and show how stupid the drunk, the robber, and the dissolute appeared to be under the searching eye of the artist. In later nineteenth-century France, Millet painted peasant people at their daily occupations. Many of his works show the people with a great natural dignity, and they are more valued today than when they were originally produced.

### Impressionism

In nineteenth-century France, a group of painters became known as the *Impressionists* because they primarily worked out-of-doors, and they tried to paint what they saw at a particular moment in time. The changing effects of water or light were a favorite subject of the Impressionists. They were concerned with the application of small amounts of pure color placed close to one another on the canvas. In this way, they believed, the viewer's eye could carry out the visual "mix" necessary for the comprehension of the visual image. Other examples of Impressionist painting can be seen in the works of Paul Cézanne, who was interested in the solidity of things. It may be noticed that in a Cézanne painting, he seems to be using blocks of color applied in square patches. Conversely, another Impressionist, Van Gogh, gave his paintings long, swirling brushstrokes which seemed to create movement in the work.

**Figure 5.8.**   Pieter de Hooch. *Interior of a Dutch House*. Reproduced by courtesy of the Trustees, The National Gallery, London.

**Figure 5.9.**    William Hogarth. *Breakfast Scene* from *Marriage a la mode*. Reproduced by courtesy of the Trustees, The National Gallery, London.

**Figure 5.10.** Jean Francois Millet. *The Sower*. Courtesy, Museum of Fine Arts, Shaw Collection.

**Figure 5.11.**   Paul Cézanne. *Mont Sainte-Victoire*. Oil on canvas. 28¾″ x 32⅛″. The Metropolitan Museum of Art. Bequest of Mrs. H. O. Havemeyer, 1929. The H. O. Havemeyer Collection.

### Pointillism

*Pointillism* was a development from Impressionism. The Pointillists were, notably, Seurat and Signac. The Pointillist painters believed that the "visual" mixing of color, first proposed by the Impressionist painters, could be even more effectively produced by the application of tiny dots of color in close proximity to one another. This, they believed, would result in an even easier visual process whereby the eye of the viewer mixed the colors visually within the retina. These examples might be shown: *Sunday Afternoon at the Grande Jatte* which was painted by Seurat in 1885; or *Felix Feneon*, painted in 1890 by Paul Signac.

**Figure 5.12.**   Georges Seurat. *Sunday Afternoon on La Grande Jatte.* Courtesy of The Art Institute of Chicago. Helen Birch Bartlett Collection.

## Cubism

There are also attempts at the representation of simultaneous viewpoints. This is common in many non-Western artists' works; but in the West it began, possibly, only with Cubism. With the Navaho sand painting and with African and Polynesian sculptures, this type of representation is common. It is usually multisided and does not have the qualities inherent in realism. The Cubist artists made a conscious attempt to show, *at one and the same moment,* several different views. Examples are seen in the painting by Duchamp titled *Nude Descending a Staircase,* of the 1913 Armory Show, or with the *Violin* series of paintings by Pablo Picasso.

*Left:*
**Figure 5.13.**    Marcel Duchamp. *Nude Descending a Staircase, No. 2.* 1912. Oil on canvas. 58″ x 35″. Philadelphia Museum of Art. The Louise and Walter Arensberg Collection.

*Page 95:*
**Figure 5.14.**    Marcel Duchamp. *Chocolate Grinder, No. 1.* 1913. Oil on canvas. 24¾″ x 25⅝″. Philadelphia Museum of Art. The Louise and Walter Arensberg Collection.

### Expressionism, or Fauvism

This is an art form which began with the French *Salon Des Refusés*. These were a group of French artists whose works were turned down for the Academy show and who thereupon set up their own exhibit. The colors they used were considered at that time to be so violent that they were called the *Fauves*, or "Wild Beasts." Examples of this type of work are *Le Cirque* (1906) by Vlaminck or the *Cypresses* of Vincent Van Gogh.

### Dadaism

The origins of the word are open to argument. The most widely held theory is that it originates from the German word for a child's rocking horse. The Dadaist movement began in Switzerland during World War I and was continued in Paris and Berlin in the 1920s. It was an art that epitomized the absurd and the unusual in a fantastic way. It sought to attack established ideas through irrational anarchistic intuition. It was pessimistic about the fate of the world. Examples might be given as Marcel Duchamp's *L.H.O.O.Q.I.G.I.G.* or his *Chocolate Grinder No. 1*.

### Surrealism

As with Dadaism, *Surrealism* is nonrational, and it deals with the magical world of the subconscious mind. The original definition of it by the French writer André Breton mentions the "omnipotence of the dream." Joan Miró, Georges Braque, and Pablo Picasso were originators who later moved into other expressive modes. Max Ernst's *The Horde*, Yves Tanguy's *The Storm*, and Salvador Dali's *The Persistence of Memory* are probable exemplars.

**Figure 5.15.** Yves Tanguy. *The Storm*. 1926. Oil on canvas. 32″ x 25¾″. Philadelphia Museum of Art. The Louise and Walter Arensberg Collection.

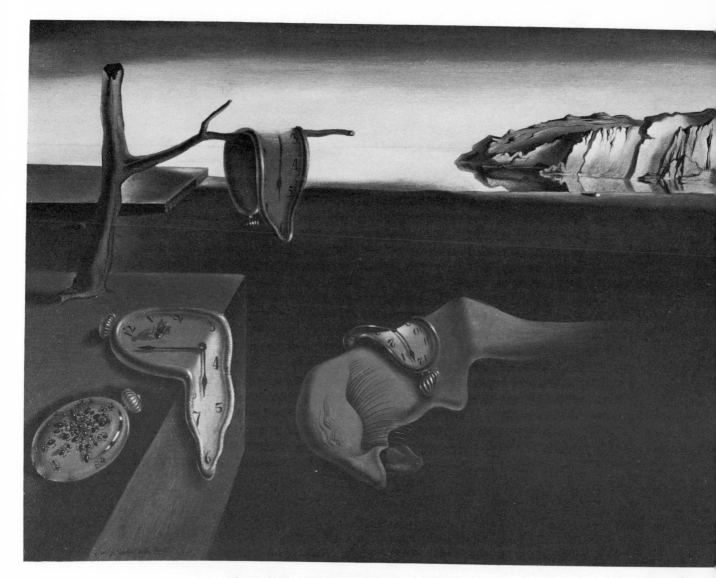

**Figure 5.16.**   Salvador Dali. *The Persistence of Memory.* 1931. Oil on canvas. 9½ x 13 inches. Collection, The Museum of Modern Art, New York.

## A Syllabus on Style in Art—Grades One Through Six

### Ways in Which the Artist Works

#### Grade 1

*Behavioral Objective.* To identify and understand the ways in which the artist works and the places in which he chooses to work.

*Presentation.* Exhibit suitable reproductions which show the various places in which art has been practiced. For example, one might show some reproductions of the paintings in Lascaux or Altamira. These are famous cave-painting sites. Similarly, one could show reproductions of primitive peoples at work on art—aboriginal Australians at work on the painting of grave posts; American Northwest Coastal

**Figure 5.17.** Vermeer. *The Artist in His Studio*. Kunsthistorisches Museum, Vienna.

Indians and their totem poles; African carvers at work on statuary; and possibly Polynesian carvers at work on canoe prows. Other kinds of outdoor work might be Egyptian or Greek statuary. Illustrations showing monk artists at work on the illumination of Medieval manuscripts would show them in their cells (or small rooms) in the monastery. Other typical reproductions might be one of Vermeer's *The Artist in His Studio*. Reproductions could show the decoration of a building as in the frescoes of Raphael or Rivera, or possibly Mosaic decoration in Byzantine churches such as Santa Apollinaire in Classe at Ravenna. Another more recent example might be that showing Monet at work in his boat as painted by Manet. Lastly, if it can be obtained, a photograph of a New York artist's loft would be of value.

**Figure 5.18.** Edouard Manet. *In the Boat*. Neve Pinakothek, Munich. SCALA—New York/Florence.

*Discussion.* The discussion would probably center upon the places in which the artists work. Questions might be phrased according to the type of accommodation under discussion:

Do you think that the size of the monk's cell had anything to do with the small-ness of the art work performed there?

Is it notable that the totem pole is a kind of work that can only be produced out-of-doors?

Why do you think the Greeks chose to make statues act as columns to support buildings?

Further questions will likely occur as the reproductions are displayed.

*Summation.* Relate the work of the class to the recent discussion. One method might be to create one or more murals (wall paintings) on large sheets of paper taped together and temporarily fastened to the wall. Another might be the creation of large sculptures out of cardboard. For example, some very creditable large-scale primitive mask shapes may be made by using large containers obtained from stores that sell appliances.

## Grade 2

*Behavioral Objective.* To examine and discuss the tools of the artist and to out-line the ways in which they may be used.

*Presentation.* For two-dimensional painting we should show illustrations or pho-tographs of the artist's palette, brushes, palette knives, canvas, and tools to make stretchers and frames. If possible, the original items might be borrowed from a local art store or art department.

*Discussion.* Discuss the brush work as seen in a painting and make comparisons. For example, talk about brush work as seen in Byzantine or Early Medieval work (such as Giotto or Masaccio) and compare these with more modern work of the Impressionists, and possibly even more recent "isms." The questions might begin with some such as these:

Do you like the pattern underlying this Byzantine painting?

Do you think the figures in *The Tribute Money* are more real than those of *The Kiss?*

Are the lights in Van Gogh's *Cafe at Night* true to life?

What happens when we look at Seurat's painting?

*Summation.* Let the children develop within their own work some of the meth-ods of brush work seen in the examples. For example, *The Bridge at Courbevoie* might encourage some members of the class to attempt a Pointillistic painting of their own. Encourage all attempts of this type, and try to provide some thick im-pasto color with which the students may experiment.

## Grade 3

*Behavioral Objective.* To familiarize the students with general information on paintings, their artists, and the general period in which they lived.

*Presentation.* Try to indicate several different schools of art by means of maps and reproductions of paintings. Show works of Early Medieval, Renaissance, French Romantic, landscape, and other types of painterly activities. Leave these

**Figure 5.19.** Georges Seurat. *The Bridge at Courbevoie*. Courtauld Institute of Art, London.

maps and related reproductions on display for some time. Encourage the students to memorize factual information. Tell them that you will be having a test on this information.

*Discussion.* Have the class discuss some of the schools of painters and the ways in which they may be recognized. Keep all this factual information of a broad and general character. Have each student write a test question and, in turn, have them pose these test questions to the group. This will be the form that the test will take, and it should not be formally graded in any way.

*Summation.* Encourage the students to read books and to look at stories about artists and their lives.

## Grade 4

*Behavioral Objective.* To make the students aware of the work of students from other countries.

*Presentation.* Try to obtain some reproductions from international art organizations. Usually the best organizations which supply material of this kind are UNESCO and The International Society for Education Through Art. There are many touring exhibitions of works by public school students from other countries which can be obtained for display, provided that advance notice is given. Having obtained some work of this nature, be sure to encourage the students to read the labels and to be aware of the approximate age range of the artists exhibiting work.

*Discussion.* Questions will naturally arise concerning the different imagery shown in the works. For example, such common everyday objects as mailboxes from another land will excite the students' curiosity. The questions should flow freely, and the teacher should be well prepared to answer them.

*Summation.* Encourage the students with an assignment to paint another country as they imagine it to be. Attempt to develop some kind of art exchange between their class and a class of students in another country. Again, this kind of thing can be very easily arranged through the international bodies already mentioned.

## Grade 5

*Behavioral Objective.* To allow the students to gain a working vocabulary about artists, their backgrounds, and the fields of art. To inspire the students to continue studying the work of artists and of particular schools and periods in art.

*Presentation.* At this time, movies, filmstrips, and slides may serve to motivate interest in artists and their work. Recent and modern examples should be displayed, and if possible, field trips to nearby museums can be organized. There should be assigned reading on famous artists, and books such as Gombrich's *The Story of Art* might be used. Mere factual information is not the main purpose of these assigned readings, but more the general enjoyment of the works and the factual background underlying them.

*Summation.* The discussion period should tie in with the work of famous men. If a film on an artist's life or the way in which he worked has been shown, try to develop student work in the studio course portion which relates to this. Encourage the students to identify, for a short time, with the work of one particular artist (possibly even to make copies of his works).

## Grade 6

*Behavioral Objective.* To have the students read about materials and techniques and discuss them in the light of their own work. To keep a logbook of principles and processes that they are using in their own art-studio experiences.

*Presentation.* Give the students assigned reports to complete. Have them bring these reports to class and deliver them orally as part of the discussion in the class period. Make reading assignments and have them read aloud to the class.

*Discussion.* Most of the discussion period should be inspired by the previous reports or lectures given. Each painting on display should also be the subject of some oral report by a student. Some questions for stimulating discussion might be the following:

What are some of the resourceful ways in which the artist has created forms?
What attitude do you think the artist had toward his objective?

What skills and technique used in this example can you see?
How does the artist express his feelings in the work?
What has made this painting famous?
What is the reason for this piece of art work remaining in existence?

*Summation.* These works and the lectures and reports should be chosen to influence the art elements and principles in the students' work. They should show students a relationship between the studio and the lecture or classroom. The students should be encouraged to express themselves clearly both in their reports and in the keeping of a logbook which sets out the methods they themselves use in the producing of art work.

# 6 the affective domain

**Feelings About Art Objects**

The discussion may be commenced with words from the teacher stressing the need to *look*. Paintings must be looked at and understood through the eyes. Students read with the eyes; in art they must learn also to "see" with the mind. A pause should be made to allow visual study of the work. A picture may show familiar things that are easy to recognize, or it may tell a story. The way it is painted may have something to do with the times in which the artist lived, and it will be more interesting if we know something about those times. The artist's feelings may be reflected in his work, and it will help to know something about him— why he painted a subject in this way and what he was thinking about. As we look at a piece of art, we find that it is not only an arrangement of colors, lines, and shapes, but also an historical document, like the Declaration of Independence, which can tell us about a subject, a country, or an individual artist.

In learning the language of pictures, we find that a great work of art has many things to say.

When we look at a work of art, we look with our eyes and with our minds. With our eyes we see the surface—the lines, the colors, and the shapes. Some make us feel excited or happy. Other colors, lines, and shapes make us feel calm or quiet. Yet others can make us feel sad. Looking only at the surface of a picture is like looking at a person without knowing what he is like "inside." Many people find that they enjoy a work of art through reading with their minds as well as just seeing the surface of it. A picture may tell how people lived in other places and times, the games they played, the food they ate, the clothes they wore, and how their homes looked both inside and outside. Sometimes it helps to understand a work if we know when the artist lived and where. Each artist creates in his own way just as everyone sees the world in his own way because we are all individuals.

The organization of the art lesson can be helpful in introducing the students to painters and paintings. One method which has been successfully adopted is to provide each student with his own personal folder in which to keep examples of work. The student chooses the name of an artist (living or dead), and this name is usually lettered by the student on to the outside of the folder. The student is then encouraged to find a reproduction of a picture painted by *himself* which is pasted on to the outside of the folder. The student goes on to find out as much as possible about *his own* life. This information is then stuck on to the inside of the folder. If these folders are used continually, it will be notable how quickly the names and the information gathered by each student are recognized and remembered. Each student can read this information to the rest of the class on selected occasions.

The visit to an art gallery or museum by a group of students can be a most disappointing experience if there has been no previous preparation. The series of lesson plans that follow this section are designed to create an enthusiasm for and a knowledge of paintings which can then be built upon by the visit to a gallery or museum. Sometimes the works of art used as examples are in the galleries and museums that are too distant to visit, even possibly in foreign places. However, in the event that teachers find it difficult or impossible to organize field trips to see original works, the use of selected reproductions, the showing of movies and other visual materials, and the use of the bibliography that follows at the end of this book will be an acceptable substitute.

When visiting a museum or gallery, there should be a period during the visit when the students should be allowed to wander through as they prefer, rather than in a large party conducted by a guide. It is far more stimulating and will lead to more interesting discussion if the students are allowed to discover certain pictures for themselves. The preparation before such a visit is important, but it is also extremely important to hold a discussion following the visit. A structured sequence during the visitation may be of preliminary value in introducing the students to the museum facilities, but the "free time" for individual visitation to different works is absolutely essential.

Students may find some embarrassment in discussing their "feelings" when looking at a work of art, particularly in the higher grades. However, if this type of discussion has proceeded from the first grade as a regular part of the art-appreciation sequence, then much of this embarrassment should be relieved.

In a recent publication, Jerome Hausman discusses the strange perceptions that occur from the almost unanimous use of slides by teachers of students for the discussion of works of art.[1] Dr. Hausman believes that the teacher using these screened images is placed, wittingly or unwittingly, in a position of certain limitations. These circumstances make for the recognition, rather than the understanding, of works of art. He suggests, further, that slides and reproductions should be used as mere "notes" in terms of the appreciation of art works. He sets up priorities. The first priority is in the matter of looking at the original and making a judgment from this looking. This would avoid the customary activity of looking at the art work and then glancing at the label to confirm the recognition when a student visits a museum. This kind of activity becomes a mere labeling and does not develop the insightful inquiry that should be part of the confrontation between the viewer and the art object.

Another contributor to the same publication suggests that the proper use of slides remains, as always, as teaching *aids*.[2] She suggests that the slides should not be changed too rapidly. She further suggests that some slides should present, sequentially, several views of the same piece of work. These views, together with explanations, will help the students with the interpretation of the work in order that they may get a better understanding.

Given the inescapable fact of the difficulty of making frequent and regular visits to a museum by many of the classes of students with whom we shall deal, the only

1. Jerome J. Hausman, "Teachers, Art Objects and Slides" *Issues in Art Education*, vol. 1, no. 7. Washington, D. C.: NAEA, pp. 1-4.
2. Diane Hopkins Hughs, *Issues in Art Education*, vol. 1, no. 7.

alternative is to use visual reproductions. It is the *manner* of the usage of these reproductions that is open to question. Provided the reproductions do not determine the type of teaching done; provided the use of slides, printed reproductions, or other visual materials do not "structure" every lesson into a format which becomes the mere recitation of factual information; provided all these pitfalls are avoided, there is nothing wrong with these materials being used. As long as the freedom of the student to depart from preconceived notions, to ask searching questions, and to *inquire* is preserved, then the integrity of the teaching remains undamaged.

## Criticizing, Appraising, and Judging— Grades One Through Six

### Feelings About an Art Object

#### Grade 1

*Behavioral Objective.* To develop an interest in art in general and in some famous works in particular. To know some of the stories behind the great works of art.

*Presentation.* Some days before the lessons, pictures that are to be discussed should be displayed in the classroom. The lesson series should be begun with an explanation that famous works of art are going to be shown through reproductions. The first few that are chosen should have interesting stories behind them so that student interest is aroused. Once a week, a period of about thirty minutes should be set aside for the introduction of these famous works. Once a week, students may bring in a picture to share with the class.

*Discussion.* The discussion could start with the following questions:

What is the artist trying to tell us?
Why do you think he painted this picture—made this print—carved this sculpture, etc.?
Do you like the colors that he used?
Do you like the picture—print—sculpture, etc.?
Do you like to paint pictures?
What do you like most about this picture—print—sculpture, etc.?

*Summation.* Give students encouragement for their own ideas and for the different things that they remark upon in the work; encourage unusual ideas; create confidence in talking about the works and make sure the students understand them. Pronounce the name of the work and the artist's name carefully for the students. Have the students repeat it until they can also pronounce it. Display the work with its title and the artist's name.

#### Grade 2

*Behavioral Objective.* To concentrate on new paintings that have to do with the children, their homes, and their friends. To relate famous works with the students' own environment by showing purpose in studying them other than for the story behind them. To have students apply what they learn to their own work as far as they can (for example, in subject matter). To have students take their work home and discuss it with their parents.

*Presentation.* Display the works for discussion for a few days where students will be sure to notice them. With this age group it will be necessary to move a little faster and not to dwell so long on one work. Anywhere from three to four paintings could be presented in a forty-five-minute discussion. As with grade one, encourage student selection of at least one example.

*Discussion.* For the discussion, keep to simple questions that may stir interest and encourage the group:

Do you see the colors of this work?
Do you paint pictures?
Why do we paint pictures?
Of what is this a picture?
Which one is your favorite?
What are works of art good for?
What kind of art do you have at home?

*Summation.* Encourage the students to use in their own personal art work subjects and colors similar to those seen. Reward such examples.

## Grade 3

*Behavioral Objective.* To encourage ideas from master works to be used in the student's own work. To develop individual interpretations. To develop awareness of locations of these original master works where they may be seen.

*Presentation.* Show a short film on some famous paintings in a particular museum. Display some famous paintings in reproduction and call attention to them from time to time. Not more than one art period a week should be taken for this activity in the third grade. Appreciation deals with media other than drawing and painting. Show some examples but do not emphasize facts alone. In the work the children are doing, try to relate this to master works on display. Make sure that the works displayed are those seen in the movie film.

*Discussion.* Talk about the appreciation of art in everyday life, using the following types of questions:

Where can one see some of these master works?
Do they have any influence on our life?
Should one know about good paintings? Why?
Where do you see a master work or a copy of one everyday?

*Summation.* Value any move the student makes to correlate his work with the works on display. Do not condemn the student for what seems to be a copy of a master work; rather, encourage this. However, if the student is discouraged when comparing his copy, encourage another, more "derived" attempt (a less literal one).

## Grade 4

*Behavioral Objective.* To relate the work of the artist to non-art topics. To show the artist as a recorder of his times. To present the work of artists of other countries.

*Presentation.* Again, the appreciation should be connected to the student work in other art areas, with emphasis on scope and breadth and different ways of creating it. Show examples that will suggest ideas to the students for similar effects.

Introduce works from non-Western countries and show examples of clothing, countries, and objects in the works selected for display. Length of presentation and discussion will depend on the interest of the group. Not less than one hour a week and no more than three periods should be taken up, as studio work is very important to this age group. Retrospective discussion of work of the past week, definitions, spelling of art terms, and works of famous artists could perhaps be a terminal lesson on Fridays.

*Discussion.* Ask questions that will bring in outside influences and other class subjects. If you can obtain a visitor from a local gallery or museum to do some of this questioning at certain periods, such a person would be an ideal "visiting discussion leader." Some suitable questions might be the following:

Why did the Africans, Chinese, American Indians, etc., work like this at this time?

Do the clothes that these people in the painting are wearing tell us anything about that period or that country?

Allow students to tell about experiences or things that they have seen or read about which they think might make a good picture. Encourage them to paint one.

*Summation.* Encourage discussion on the different cultural perceptions of a society and/or a world; for example, Chinese "perspective," African "abstract figurative" sculptures, Navaho sand paintings.

## Grade 5

*Behavioral Objective.* To look at works of variety. To provide challenges to ideas and opinions of art.

*Presentation.* Place dramatic pictures on display in the room. A simplified textbook should be used at this level, and weekly readings might be assigned. Two periods a week might be spent on appreciation, with three days of studio work alternating with two days of appreciation. This should correlate students' techniques with those of the work on display.

*Discussion.* Some questions that might be asked would be these:

Why were these colors used?

Does this picture make you feel cold or warm? How?

Which picture would you most like to be a part of? Why?

Describe the background. Why do you think the artist used this type?

Does this explain to us the way of life during this period?

Encourage the students to make a self-evaluation in terms of their knowledge of art. Ask what things they would like to study and try to select appropriate works.

*Summation.* Praise the student for his contributions to discussions. Encourage the student to correlate his work with that displayed. With each student, begin the use of the notebook for recording "good ideas."

## Grade 6

*Behavioral Objective.* To give reading material on artists and to encourage study of it. To encourage individual identification with one artist.

*Presentation.* On a reading shelf, place books on life stories of famous artists. Give library reading credit to students who read these books. Continue to display work that is to be discussed. Assign each student to a "named artist" (preferably of the student's own choice) and require collection of reproductions by each student "biographer." Have the students take turns in making a report to the class about "their" artists. Different students should read about and study reproductions. The student should conduct the discussion on "his" artist and on the selections others have studied and may question.

*Discussion.* Since the students will be conducting the discussions, it is the teacher's sole responsibility to keep the class at attention and involved. When discussion lags, the teacher may insert provocative questions that will stimulate further dialogue:

Was the artist a happy man?
Was the artist famous when he was painting?
Why did the artist move around so much?
What kind of a home did the artist come from?
What made this artist so famous?

*Summation.* The students should be aware of the techniques that the artist used, and perhaps they, too, can use these same techniques. The student biographers should plan each exhibit of famous art reproductions for the individual artist under examination. The continuation of the notebook on "good ideas" should be enriched by knowledge of individual artist's methods of work.

## Art Appreciation Is Sensitivity Training

The art-teaching profession is turning again to the task of inculcating aesthetic sensitivities. So, for that matter, is the federal government. At a time of tremendous fiscal stringency, Congress has consistently supported increased endowment for the Arts. This is not a new phenomenon, of course, since one of the greatest and most productive periods of government support for the Arts was during the later depression years. Recent issues of the journals of art education have publicized an increasing number of opinions on the aesthetic component of education. Art-teaching in this country has moved from learning by doing, through the self-expressive and therapeutic, through the development of training as consumers, to concern for our surroundings. These humanitarian concerns all demand a critical appraisal of what art and the artist are all about. McLuhan's statement, "Art is anything you can get away with," has the corollary that it would be beneficial to all of us if we understood what the artist is "getting away with."

A surgeon cannot develop his skill merely by casual observation of hospital patients. The critical faculties needed for appreciating art cannot be developed from infrequent and nondirected encounters with works in museums and galleries. Many art teachers tend to draw upon their own experience in college and adopt an "art history" approach to the problem. This alone is not enough. However, some art knowledge and information should be given almost as a rote-learning sequence. It will become useful bedrock upon which to erect a structure of judgment, understanding, and appreciation. This factual importance demands accuracy and understandable language to make it a valid experience.

Together with this factual presentation, however, must come those activities such as are described in this book. In this way the two sets of learning will provide for the education of sensitive individuals.

Appreciation is an intensely personal activity, even when all the advice and indoctrination are absorbed. The child (and, later, the adult) will yet base criticism and appreciation on purely subjective reactions. Art teachers developing programs such as those suggested, however, can provide a broader basis for criticism. The development of the children's art judgment makes their vision of the world richer and more expansive and their perceptions more objective.

That is the purpose of this book.

# a list of art words

Abstract art. The making of pictures or sculptures which have no likeness to natural or known objects.

Abstract Expressionism. Action painting (tachisme). The dripping or splattering of paint on to a canvas to produce a special effect.

Academic. A way of working to rules and customs in art. Unoriginal work.

Academy. A place to study art.

Acropolis. The citadel or hilltop part of a Greek city.

Aerial perspective. The use of colder or paler colors for distant objects.

*Alla prima (Aller preema)*. Italian words meaning the completion of a painting with one layer of paint at one time.

Altarpiece. A painting above and behind an altar, often in sections.

Appliqué. A pattern or picture formed by cut-out materials.

Aquarelle. A drawing or print colored by watercolor washes.

Aquatint. A type of print made by dipping a plate in acid to etch it.

Architecture. The design and construction of buildings according to use or need.

Armature. A wire or metal support for a clay model.

Assemblage (Ass-om-blarge). Arrangement of objects to make a visual three-dimensional composition.

Asymmetry (As-simm-ettree). Irregular but orderly arrangement of objects of different size and shape on either side of a central point. Opposite to symmetry.

Anatomy. The study of the bones and muscles of the human figure.

Background. In a picture, the most distant section.

Balance. Art elements that are of equal weight or importance and arranged in an orderly manner in a picture or design.

Baroque (Barr-oak). A style of art in Europe that used dramatic, swirling composition or decoration.

Bas-relief (Bar-relief). A shape that rises from a background, as with the head on a coin.

Bauhaus (Bough-house). A German design school which tried to link art, science, and engineering.

Biscuit. Pottery after one baking at moderate heat only.

Brayer. A rubber roller used for inking printing blocks.

Broken color. Color varied by other colors.

Calligraphy. Beautiful handwriting, *or*, the use of a free-flowing line in a drawing or painting.

Caricature. A drawing of a person which exaggerates the features.

Cartoon. A humorous drawing. In older times, the artist's first sketch for a large picture.

Casting. A mold-made sculpture. A duplication.

Ceramics. The changing of damp clay objects to useful objects by baking in a special oven, or kiln.

Chiaroscuro. Light and shade in a picture.

Cloisonné (Cloyzonay). Design made of little metal walls with colored enamels filling the spaces between. It is then baked or fired in a kiln.

Collage (Collarge). A design or picture made from fragments of all kinds of different materials.

Color. One of the elements of art, produced by light entering the eye. Value varies from light to dark, and intensity varies from bright to dull.

Composition. The organizing or putting together of the elements of an art work.

Constructivism. Sculptures made from metal, wood, wire, etc. Usually abstract.

Contrast. Putting opposite elements close together to make a design more exciting.

Cool colors. Green, blue, and similar colors.

Crafts. Useful objects, usually hand-made, original and beautiful in design.

Cubism. A reduction of the parts of an object to basic shapes such as squares, rectangles, cylinders, or discs. The showing of several different sides of an object at one and the same time in the same picture.

Dadaism (Day-duh-ism) The combining of non-art objects, often in an unplanned way, as a protest against the rules or traditions of art and society.

Design. The arrangement of a work of art. A plan or the making of a plan of work.

Dry brush. Loading a brush with tempera, partially squeezing it dry, and then lightly passing it across the paper or canvas.

Dry point. A way of scratching a design on a metal plate which is then inked and printed.

Engraving. Cutting lines on wood or metal blocks or plates for printing.

Etching. Cutting lines in a metal plate by allowing acid to reach certain parts of the plate. These lines hold ink and will print on paper when squeezed in a press.

Expressionism. A kind of picture which shows deep emotion by its choice of colors and shapes.

Eye level or eye line (or horizon line). In perspective, the line in front of the viewer's eye. Where sky meets ground outdoors. Where lines meet. Also seen in interior views.

Facade (Fass-ard). Front of a building, often decorated.

Fauvism (Fove-ism). From fauves—wild beasts. French newspapers used this to describe a group of painters who in 1905 used violent, brilliant colors in their work.

Fixative. A transparent varnish which is sprayed on pencil, chalk, or pastel drawings to prevent smudging.

Foreground. The lower part of a picture that seems to be closer to the viewer.

Foreshortening. The artist's way of drawing an object that is pointing directly at the viewer's eye. It appears shorter than it is.

Form. An element of art, sometimes meaning shape, sometimes mass.

Fresco. Painting on plaster: When dry—*fresco seco;* When wet—*buon fresco.*

Futurism. An Italian group who tried to show movement and action in their works.

Genre (Djon-ruh). A scene from everyday life.

Gesso (Jess-o). Plaster of paris, or gypsum. Used to prepare a surface for painting.

Glaze. A transparent film of color in a painting; or, a special hard finish applied to clay objects baked in a kiln. (*See* Ceramics).

Gothic. A style of painting, sculpture, and architecture in Northern Europe between 1100 and 1400. Arches were pointed; walls were thin and supported by extra buttresses.

Gouache (Goo-ash). Opaque colors, mixed with gum and tempered with white. The paper does not show through (as in watercolor or aquarelle).

Halftone (or middle tone). A value halfway between dark and light.

Highlight. Any surface catching the most light. The "shiniest" parts of an object.

Icon. A religious painting of Eastern Europe.

Iconography (Ike-onoggraffee). The visual language of symbols and signs.

Illumination. Decorating the pages of a book, especially capital letters, with color or gold leaf.

Illustration. Commercial drawings or pictures which "tell a story," usually in magazines or books.

Impasto. Thick paint applied so that it hardens into marks and ridges made by the knife or brush that was used.

Impressionism. A style of painting which was done on the spot rather than in a studio. It attempted to capture an atmosphere or light-filled impression of a scene and used spectrum colors with no black or brown.

Line. One of the elements of art.

Linear perspective. The art of showing solid objects on a flat plane by using the science of perspective.

Lithography (Lie-thog-raffee). Printing by means of marking on a limestone block or zinc plate with a greasy crayon. This attracts ink which does not "take" on the rest of the surface. Pulled on a press, it prints the design on a sheet of paper.

Local color. The positive color of an object unaffected by other things such as light.

Mass. An element of art form. Opposite of space.

Media, Medium. The material of an art work, for example, oil paint is a medium.

Mobile. A kind of hanging sculpture made of shapes which move around one another.

Monochrome. Single-color work.

Mosaic. A design or picture made by fixing tiles, glass, etc., to a wall or similar surface.

Mural. A large wall painting.

Negative space. The space between two or more positive shapes or masses, such as sky between trees.

Neutral color. Paint made by grinding pigments in oil.

Nonobjectivism. *See* Abstract.

Oil color. Paint made by grinding pigments in oil.

Opaque color (Opake). Nontransparent color. Tempera is opaque.

Painting. An art work made in any of the painting media. It need not be a picture if it has no subject.

Palette. The flat board on which the artist mixes his colors; *or*, the complete range of colors used by an artist or group of artists.

Pastel. Dry pigments, usually in stick form.

Pastiche (Pas-teesh). Art that merely imitates the art of others.

Patina (Par-teener). Copper turns green after awhile, while other metals redden with rust. Wood develops a "skin"—all these are examples of a "patina."

Pattern. A decorative design, the parts of which are repeated again and again.

Perspective. *See* Aerial and Linear perspective.

Pigment. The powder that, when mixed, forms a color.

Plane. A level surface.

Pointillism. A style of painting made up of many separate dots of pure color, placed close together. The viewer tends to "mix" them by eye if he looks from the correct distance.

Portrait. An artist's rendering of a person's features.

Poster. A commercial design used to advertise.

Poster color. Opaque watercolor, usually in tubes or pots.

Powder color. Opaque watercolor in powder form.

Primary colors. Red, yellow, and blue, from which it is possible to mix most of the other colors.

Print. An impression made from an inked block or plate on to a sheet of paper. A "positive" photograph processed from negative film.

Proportion. Relationships of size or importance in natural or human forms.

Realism. The story of contemporary life so as, visually, to "tell it like it is."

Renaissance (Renn-ace-annce). Rebirth of interest in classic art that began in the 1300s in Italy.

Rhythm. One of the visual principles. Repeating of an element in an art work.

Romanticism. Art based upon imagination or, often, a memory.

School. A group of workers or artists who seemed to have similar ideas and methods.

Sculpture. Three-dimensional work which can be subtractive (carved or cut away); additive (built up in layers); or constructive (joined together).

Shape. One of the elements of art form.

Sketch. A quick drawing or painting which can be an idea for another work *or* may be complete as it is.

Slip. Mixed water and clay used by potters.

Still life. A subject or arrangement for a picture of nonliving objects.

Study. A careful drawing or painting, often in preparation for a further work.

Style. The recognizable manner of an artist's work.

Surrealism (Sir-realizzum). Art based upon dreams and fantasy. Extremely accurate reproduction of objects yet a surprise to the viewer because they are not usually seen together. Superrealistic art.

Symmetry (Sim-mettree). Balancing of one shape or form with a similar one.

Tachism (Tashizzum). *See* Action painting.

Taste. A person's own idea of what is pleasing to him. Not to be confused with art judgment.

Tempera. Opaque color mixed with water and a "binding" ingredient.

Terra-cotta. Hard, unglazed ceramics of a reddish-brown color.

Tessera (Tes-sera). Smallest part of a Mosaic.

Texture. Roughness, smoothness, or graininess of a surface.

Throwing. The potter's way of forming a clay vessel on a revolving potter's wheel.

Tooth. The roughness or grain of canvas or board used in painting.

Transparent. Opposite of opaque. A transparent color does not hide the surface below it. Aquarelle (or watercolor) is transparent.

Triptych (Trip-titch). An altarpiece consisting of three leaves, or panels, each with a painting on it.

Trompe-l'oeuil (Tromp loy). A picture that creates an illusion. The artist uses a trick to deceive the eye by making a painted object appear to be added to the picture. For example, a viewer might imagine a painted drop of water, or an insect, to be removable from the canvas. These French words mean "to deceive the eye."

Unity. All the elements in a work arranged in a harmonious fashion. Color unity is seen when all those used come from the warm or cool areas of the spectrum.

Value. The amount of light, or dark, in a color.

Vanishing point. In linear perspective, the point on the eye level or horizon at which parallel lines appear to meet and vanish.

Vignette (Veen-yet). An ornament of leaves on a building or a decorated capital letter in a book or a small picture which has an irregular edge within the arrangement of a book page.

Visual meaning. Something which is well expressed in visual, rather than verbal, terms.

Vorticism (Vorteesizzum). Similar to Futurism. An attempt to bring all art into line with the "age of the machine."

Warm colors. Opposite in the spectrum to cool colors. For example, yellow is a warm color.

Wash. A thin layer of aquarelle, or watercolor paint, which covers a large area. The artist refers to "laying a wash."

Watercolor. Pure watercolor is usually described by this term (*see also* Aquarelle) and is transparent. When white is added, it becomes opaque and is usually referred to as *gouache*. Poster colors are also opaque watercolors.

Wedges. Triangular pieces of wood which are hammered into slots in the inside corners of a canvas frame or stretcher. They serve to stretch the canvas more tightly.

Woodcut. A print made from a wooden block, cut so that the relief parts print the design. The unwanted parts are cut away and do not print.

Wood engraving. Similar to a wood block but usually containing a more complicated arrangement of lines and grooves which will make the finished print.

# bibliography
# of visual resources

Harry N. Abrams, 110 East 59th Street, New York, New York 10022. (Color reproductions)

ACI Films, Inc., 16 West 46th Street, New York, New York 10036. (Films on art)

American Book Company, 450 West 33rd Street, New York, New York 10001. (Multipurpose laminated art prints—guide booklets, etc.)

American Council on Education, 1785 Massachusetts Avenue, N.W. Washington, D.C. 20063. (Slides and filmstrips)

American Crafts Council, Research and Education Department, 29 West 53rd Street, New York, New York 10019. (Films, filmstrips on art)

American Federation of Arts, 41 East 65th Street, New York, New York 10021. (Exhibitions, films, prints, reproductions—special art curriculum—visual units)

American Handicrafts Company, 83 West Van Buren Street, Chicago, Illinois 60605. (Films)

American Library Color Slide Company, 305 East 45th Street, New York, New York 10017. (Slides in units of 10—art in retrospect)

Art Council Aids, Box 641, Beverly Hills, California 90213. (Slides and filmstrips)

Art Education, Inc., Blauvelt, New York 10913. (Color reproductions)

Artext Prints, Inc., Westport, Connecticut 06880. (Color reproductions)

Associated American Artists, Inc., 663 Fifth Avenue, New York, New York 10022. (Color reproductions)

Audio Film Center, 34 MacQuesten Parkway South, Mount Vernon, New York 10550. (Classic films)

Audio Film Center, 406 Clement Street, San Francisco, California 94118. (Classic films)

Audio Film Center, 1619 North Cherokee, Los Angeles, California 90028. (Classic films)

Audio Film Center, 8615 Directors' Row, Dallas, Texas 75247. (Classic films)

Audio Film Center, 512 Burlington Avenue, LaGrange, Illinois 60525. (Classic films)

Audio Visual Center, Indiana University, Bloomington, Indiana 47401. (Films, filmstrips, etc., rental or purchase on art, architecture, archaeology, anthropology)

Audio Visual Center, University of Kentucky, Lexington, Kentucky 40506. (Films on art, architecture, anthropology, archaeology, etc.)

Bailey-Film Associates, 11559 Santa Monica Blvd., Los Angeles, California 90025. (Slides and filmstrips)

B.F.A. Educational Media, (Columbia Broadcasting System), 2211 Michigan Avenue, Santa Monica, California 90404. (16mm films on art, perception, etc.)

Birren Color Slides. For address, *see* Van Nostrand Reinhold Co. (The vision of color—32 slides with manual. The perception of color—32 slides with manual.)

Dr. Block Color Productions, 1309 North Genessee Avenue, Los Angeles, California 90046. (Slides and filmstrips)

Brandon Films, Inc., 221 West 57th Street, New York, New York 10019. (Films)

British Information Services, 30 Rockefeller Plaza, New York, New York 10020. (Films)

Budek Films and Slides, 1023 Waterman Avenue, East Providence, Rhode Island 02914; or P.O. Box 307, Santa Barbara, California 93102. (Color slides, filmstrips, and films)

Burns and MacEachern, Ltd., 62 Railside Road, Don Mills, Ontario, Canada. (Canadian representatives for Praeger/Phaidon, etc.)

Carnegie-Mellon University, College of Fine Arts, Schenley Park, Pittsburgh, Pennsylvania 15213. (Slides and films)

Center for Cassette Studies, 8110 Webb Avenue, N. Hollywood, California 91605. (Cassette recordings on art, related subjects)

Center for Humanities, Inc., 2 Holland Avenue, White Plains, New York 10603. (Sound-Slide sets on art)

Center for Mass Communication of Columbia University Press, 562 West 113th Street, New York, New York 10025. (Films, tapes, recordings on art, etc.)

Chelsea House Publishers—The University at Large. (Rental, purchase films. Artists/critics on selected topics.)

Churchill Films, 662 North Robertson Blvd., Los Angeles, California 90069. (Films)

Classics Exchange. (Films)

Coast Visual Education Company, 5620 Hollywood Blvd., Los Angeles, California 90028. (Films)

Columbia Cinamatheque, 711 Fifth Avenue, New York, New York 10022. (Films)

Contemporary Films, Inc., 330 West 42nd Street, New York, New York 10036. (Films)

Contemporary Films/McGraw-Hill, Princeton Road, Hightstown, New Jersey 08520.

Contemporary Films/McGraw-Hill, 828 Custer Avenue, Evanston, Illinois 60702.

Contemporary Films/McGraw-Hill, 1714 Stockton Street, San Francisco 94133. (Rental/purchase films on art, related subjects)

Educational Audio Visual, Inc., Pleasantville, New York 10570. (Films, overhead transparencies, filmstrip, sound filmstrips, slides, tapes, cassettes, on fine arts, etc.)

Educational Dimensions Corporation, Box 488, Great Neck, New York 11022. (Color sound filmstrips Understanding art, perception, various topics)

Encyclopedia Britannica Films, Inc., 425 North Michigan Avenue, Chicago, Illinois 60611. (Films)

Film Classics Exchange, 1645 North La Brea Avenue, Los Angeles, California 90028. (Films)

Film Distribution Section, Colonial Williamsburg Foundation, Box C, Williamsburg, Virginia 23185. (Slides) ˜

Film Distributor Corporation, 43 West 16th Street, New York, New York 10011. (Films on art)

Films Inc., 1144 Wilmette Avenue, Wilmette, Illinois 60091. (Technicolor sound film cartridges on art, perception, etc.)

Francis Thompson Productions, 935 Second Avenue, New York, New York 10022. (Films)

General Electric Educational Films, 70 Washington Avenue, Schenectady, New York 12305. (Films on color, light, optics)

Girl Scouts of America Film Library, 830 Third Avenue, New York, New York 10022. (Films)

Grolier Educational Corporation, 845 Third Avenue, New York, New York 10022. (Slides and filmstrips)

The Jan Handa Organization, 2821 East Grand Blvd., Detroit, Michigan 48211. (Color filmstrips and synchronized records)

Harmon Foundation, Division of Visual Experiments, 140 Nassau Street, New York, New York 10038. (Films)

Harry Hester and Associates, 11422 Harry Hines Blvd., Dallas, Texas 75229. (Single concept color standard or super 8mm film loops, filmstrips, cassette tapes)

Homer Groening, 301 Executive Building, Portland, Oregon 97204. (Films)

Indian Arts and Crafts Board, Department of the Interior, The Tipi Shop, Inc., Box 1270, Rapid City, South Dakota 57701. (Color slide lecture kits on Indian crafts, painting)

International Film Bureau, Inc., 332 South Michigan Avenue, Chicago, Illinois 60604. (Color films and filmstrips—Euro and Canadian Subsidiaries)

Janus Films, 745 Fifth Avenue, New York, New York 10022. (Classic films for rental or purchase)

Jeff Dell Film Service, Inc., 1150 Avenue of the Americas, New York, New York 10036. (Films)

Kennedy Graphics, Inc., 20 East 56th Street, New York, New York 10022. (Edition Olympia art posters on Olympic Games)

Latin American Audio Visual Materials, P392 Pan American Development Foundation, 17th St. and Constitution Avenue, N.W., Washington, D.C. 20006. (Slides on Latin American art, crafts, etc.)

Life Filmstrips, Time-Life Building, Rockefeller Center, New York, New York 10020. (Slides and filmstrips)

McGraw-Hill, 330 West 42nd Street, New York, New York 10036. (Slides and filmstrips)

McGraw-Hill Films, 327 West 42nd Street, New York, New York 10036. (Films, filmstrips on art for K-12 usage)

Mass Media Ministries, 1720 Chouteau Avenue, St. Louis, Missouri 63103. (Films on art/religion, filmstrips)

Metropolitan Museum of Art Book and Art Shop, Fifth Avenue & 82nd Street, New York, New York 10028. (Color reproductions)

Miniature Gallery, 60 Rushett Close, Long Ditton, Surrey KT7 OUT England. (Color slides)

Monument Film Corporation, 267 West 25th Street, New York, New York 10001. (Films on artists)

Museum of Modern Art, 11 West 53rd Street, New York, New York 10019. (Films on art. Classic films and others.)

My Weekly Reader—Art Gallery, Education Center, Columbus, Ohio 43216. (Reproductions—teachers guide booklet)

National Film Board of Canada, 400 West Madison Street, Chicago, Illinois 60606. (Films)

National Gallery of Art, Constitution Avenue & 6th Street N.W., Washington, D.C. 20001. (Slides and filmstrips)

NBC News. (Films on Art. Commentator—Aline Saarinen)

New York Graphic Society, 140 Greenwich Avenue, Greenwich, Connecticut 06830. (Color reproductions)

N.I.T., Bureau of Audio Visual Education, School of Education, Indiana University, Bloomington, Indiana 47401. (TV video tape programs—"Images and Things")

Northern Illinois University, Division of Communications Services, DeKalb, Illinois 60115. (Films, etc., on art, etc.)

Oestreicher's Prints, Inc., 43 West 46th Street, New York, New York 10036. (Color reproductions)

Pan American Development Foundation, 7th St. & Constitution Avenue, N.W., Washington, D.C. 20006. (South American art-slides-16mm color sound films)

Penn Print Company, 572 Fifth Avenue, New York, New York 10036. (Color reproductions)

Pennsylvania Gallery of Fine Arts, Broad and Cherry Streets, Philadelphia, Pennsylvania 19102. (Slides of Museum's collection)

Philadelphia Museum of Art, Division of Education, 25th Street and Benjamin Franklin Pkwy., Philadelphia, Pennsylvania 19130. (Slides and filmstrips)

Pictura Films Distribution Corporation, 43 West 16th Street, New York, New York 10011. (Films on art)

Portafilms, 4180 Dixie Highway, Drayton Plains, Michigan 48020. (Films)

Dr. Konrad Prothmann, 2378 Soper Avenue, Baldwin, New York 11510. (Slides and filmstrips)

Raymond and Raymond, Inc., 1071 Madison Avenue, New York, New York 10028. (Color reproductions)

Red Parrot Films Ltd., 32 East 69th Street, New York, New York 10021. (Films on artists at work)

Reinhold Publishing Company, 430 Park Avenue, New York, New York 10022. (Color reproductions)

Research and Education Department. (*See* American Craftsmen's Council)

Sandak, Inc., 4 East 48th Street, New York, New York 10017. (Slides and filmstrips)

Santa Fe Film Bureau, 80 East Jackson Blvd., Chicago, Illinois 60604. (Films)

School of the Art Institute of Chicago, South Michigan Avenue and East Adams Street, Chicago, Illinois 60603. (Slides and filmstrips)

Shorewood Reproductions, Inc., Department 2, 724 Fifth Avenue, New York, New York 10019. (Color reproductions)

Sigma Educational Films, P.O. Box 1235, Studio City, California 91604. (Films)

Skira Art Books, dist. by World Publishing Company, 2231 West 110th Street, Cleveland, Ohio 44102. (Color reproductions)

Society for Visual Education, Inc., 1345 Diversey Pkwy., Chicago, Illinois 60614. (Slides and filmstrips)

Sterling Movies, 375 Park Avenue, New York, New York 10022. (Films)

Thorne Films, Inc., 1229 University Avenue, Boulder, Colorado 80302. (Slides and filmstrips)

Tiger Productions, 3559 Cody Road, Sherman Oaks, California 91403. (Films)

UNESCO, Place de Fontenoy, Paris 7e, France. (Catalog of color reproductions)

UNESCO Catalogues, Columbia University Press, 440 West 110th Street, New York, New York 10025. (Color reproductions)

University Galleries, Department SA, 520 Fifth Avenue, New York, New York 10036. (Color reproductions)

University Prints, 15 Brattle Street, Harvard Square, Cambridge, Massachusetts 02138. (Slides and filmstrips)

University of Southern California, Audio-Visual Services, Department of Cinema, 3518 University Avenue, Los Angeles, California 90007. (Films)

Van Nostrand Reinhold Company, 450 West 33rd Street, New York, New York 10001. (Color slides, Reinhold visuals)

Visual Education, Inc., P.O. Box 6039, Santa Barbara, California 93111. (Silent super 8mm film loops)

Visual Media for the Arts and Humanities, Box 137, Cherry Hill, New Jersey 08003. (Slides in sets, filmstrips on art)

Wanami Films, Japan. (Films)

Warren Schloat Productions, Inc., Pleasantville, New York 10570. (Color sound film strips on artists at work, art and art history single concept, silent standard 8, Super 8 f/loops)

Weston Woods Studios, Weston, Connecticut 06880. (Films)

E. Weyhe, 794 Lexington Avenue, New York, New York 10021. (Color reproductions)

Yellow Ball Workshop and Newton Mini Films, 62 Tarbell Avenue, Lexington, Massachusetts 02173. (Films)

# bibliography
# of book resources

ADLER, IRVING. *Color in Your Life.* New York: John Day, 1962.

ALEXANDRIAN, SARANE. *Surrealist Art.* New York: Praeger Publishers, Inc., 1970.

ALLEN, AGNES. *The Story of Sculpture.* New York: Roy Publishers, Inc., Nd.

ANDERSON, DONALD M. *Elements of Design.* New York: Holt, Rinehart & Winston, Inc., 1961.

ANDREWS, MICHAEL F. *Aesthetic Form and Education.* Syracuse, N.Y.: Syracuse University Press, 1958.

ARNHEIM, RUDOLPH. *Art and Visual Perception.* 4th ed. Berkeley: University of California Press, 1964.

ARNOLD, SIR THOMAS W. *Painting in Islam: A Study of the Place of Pictorial Art in Muslim Culture.* New York: Dover Publications, Inc., 1928.

BACH, ROBERT O., ed. *Communication: The Art of Understanding and Being Understood.* New York: Hastings House, Publishers, 1963.

BAIGELL, MATTHEW. *A History of American Painting.* New York: Praeger Publishers, Inc., 1971.

BALDINGER, WALLACE S. *The Visual Arts.* Rev. ed. New York: Holt, Rinehart & Winston, Inc., 1963.

BALLINGER, LOUISE B., and VROMAN, THOMAS F. *Design: Sources and Resources.* New York: Reinhold Publishing Corp., 1965.

BARNES, ALBERT C. *The Art in Painting.* New York: Harcourt, Brace & World, 1937.

BARR, ALFRED. *Masters of Modern Art.* New York: Museum of Modern Art. 1959.

———. *What Is Modern Painting?* New York: Museum of Modern Art, 1958.

BARRY, GERALD. *The Arts: Man's Creative Imagination.* New York: Doubleday & Co., Inc., 1965.

BATE, NORMAN. *When Cavemen Painted.* New York: Charles Scribner's Sons, 1963.

BAUMANN, HANS. *The Caves of the Great Hunters.* New York: Pantheon Books, Inc., 1962.

BAUMGART, FRITZ. *A History of Architectural Styles.* New York: Praeger Publishers, Inc., 1970.

BAZIN, GERMAIN. *Baroque and Rococo Art.* New York: Praeger Publishers, Inc., 1964.

BERENSON, BERNARD. *The Italian Painters of the Renaissance.* 2 vols. New York: Praeger Publishers, Inc., Phaidon Press Books, 1968.

BERGERE, THEA, and BERGERE, RICHARD. *From Stones to Skyscrapers.* New York: Dodd, Mead & Co., 1960.

BERGER, RENE. *The Language of Art.* London: Thames & Hudson, 1963.

BERRY, ANA M. *Art for Children.* New York: Studio-Crowell, 1952.

———. *First Book of Paintings.* New York: Franklin Watts, Inc., 1960.

BETHERS, RAY. *Composition in Pictures.* 2nd ed. New York: Pitman Publishing Corp., 1962.

———. *How Paintings Happen.* New York: W. W. Norton Co., Inc. 1951.

———. *Pictures, Paintings, and You,* New York: Pitman Publishing Corp., Nd.

BINYON, LAURENCE. *Paintings in the Far East.* 3rd ed. New York: Dover Publications, Inc., 1923.

———. *Persian Miniature Painting.* New York: Dover Publications, Inc., 1967.

BIRREN, FABER. *Color: A Survey in Words and Pictures.* Hyde Park, N.Y.: University Books, Inc., 1963.

BLAKE, PETER. *God's Own Junkyard: The Planned Deterioration of America's Landscape.* New York: Holt, Rinehart & Winston, Inc., 1964.

———. *The Master Builders.* New York: Alfred A. Knopf, Inc., 1960.

BLESH, RUDI. *Modern Art U.S.A.* New York: Alfred A. Knopf, Inc., 1956.

BOARDMAN, JOHN. *Greek Art.* New York: Praeger Publishers, Inc., 1964.

BORRISON, MARY JO. *Let's Go to an Art Museum.* New York: G. P. Putnam's Sons, 1960.

BORTEN, HELEN. *Do You See What I See?* New York: Abelard-Schuman, 1959.

———. *A Picture Has a Special Look.* New York: Abelard-Schuman, 1961.

BOWNESS, ALAN. *Contemporary British Painting.* New York: Praeger Publishers, Inc., 1968.

BROWN, MARGARET WISE. *The House of a Hundred Windows.* New York: Harper & Row, Publishers, 1945.

BROWNER, RICHARD. *Look Again.* New York: Atheneum Publishers, 1962.

BRUMME, LUDWIG C. *American Sculpture.* New York: Crown Publishers, Inc., 1948.

BRUSTLEIN, DANIEL. *The Magic Stones.* New York: McGraw-Hill Book Co., 1957.

CAMPBELL, ELIZABETH. *Fins and Tails.* Boston: Little, Brown & Co., 1963.

CANADAY, JOHN. *Keys to Art.* New York: Tudor Publishing Co., 1963.

———. *Mainstreams of Modern Art.* New York: Holt, Rinehart & Winston, Inc., 1959.

CANE, FLORENCE. *The Artist in Each of Us.* New York: Pantheon Books, Inc., 1951.

CARY, JOYCE. *Art and Reality: Ways of the Creative Process.* Garden City, N.Y.: Doubleday & Co., Inc., Anchor Books, 1961.

CASTEDO, LEOPOLDO. *A History of Latin American Art and Architecture.* Translated by Phyllis Freeman. New York: Praeger Publishers, Inc., 1969.

CELENDER, DONALD. *Musical Instruments in Art.* Minneapolis: Lerner Publications Co., 1966.

CHAET, BERNARD. *Artists at Work.* Cambridge: Hill & Wang, Inc., Webb Books, 1960.

CHANDLER, ANNA, *Story Lives of Master Artists.* Rev. ed. New York: J. B. Lippincott Co., 1953.

CHASE, A. ELIZABETH. *Famous Paintings.* New York: Platt & Munk, 1964.

CHENEY, SHELDON. *A Primer of Modern Art.* New York: Tudor Publishing Co., 1951.

———. *Expressionism in Art.* New York: Liveright, 1941.

———. *A New World History of Art.* New York: Holt, Rinehart & Winston, Inc., 1956.

CHRISTENSEN, ERWIN. *Primitive Art.* New York: Crown Publishers, Inc., Bonanza Books, 1955.

COEN, RENA NEUMANN. *American History in Art.* Minneapolis: Lerner Publications Co., 1965.

———. *Kings and Queens in Art.* Minneapolis: Lerner Publications Co., 1964.

*Contemporary American Painting and Sculpture.* 4 vols. Urbana: University of Illinois Press, 1965-69.

COOMARASWAMY, ANANDA K. *History of Indian and Indonesian Art.* New York: Dover Publications, Inc., Nd.

COOPER, DOUGLAS. *The Cubist Epoch.* New York: Praeger Publishers, Inc., Phaidon Press Art Books, 1971.

COPPLESTONE, TREWIN. *Modern Art Movements.* New York: International Publications Service, Marboro Books, 1967.

CORNELIUS, SUE, and CORNELIUS, CHASE. *The City in Art.* Minneapolis: Lerner Publications Co., 1965.

CRAVEN, THOMAS. *The Rainbow Book of Art.* Cleveland: World Publishing Co., 1956.

———. *Men of Art.* New York: Simon & Schuster, 1931.

DALY, KATHLEEN N. *Colors.* New York: Western Publishing Co., Inc., Golden Press, 1959.

DART-POUSETTE, NATHANIEL. *American Painting Today.* New York: Hastings House Publishers, 1956.

DE BORHEGYI, SUZANNE. *Museums: A Book to Begin On.* New York: Holt, Rinehart & Winston, Inc., 1962.

DUGGAN, ALFRED. *Arches and Spires.* New York: Random House, Inc., Pantheon Books, Inc., 1962.

ECKER, DAVID W. *Improving the Teaching of Art Appreciation.* Washington, D. C.: U. S. Department of Health, Education and Welfare, November 1966.

EDMAN, IRWIN. *Arts and the Man.* New York: W. W. Norton & Co., Inc., 1939.

ELIOT, ALEXANDER. *Three Hundred Years of American Painting.* New York: Time, Inc., 1957.

ELSEN, ALBERT E. *Purposes of Art.* New York: Holt, Rinehart & Winston, Inc., 1967.

ELUARD, PAUL. *Pablo Picasso.* New York: Philosophical Library, Inc., 1947.

FAULKNER, RAY, and ZIEGFELD, EDWIN. *Art Today.* 5th ed. New York: Holt, Rinehart & Winston, Inc., 1969.

FAURE, ELIE. *History of Art*. 5 vols. Translated by Walter Pach. New York: Harper & Row, 1921-30.

FELDMAN, EDMUND B. *Art as Image and Idea*, Englewood Cliffs, N. J.: Prentice-Hall, Inc., 1967.

FENOLLOSA, ERNEST F. *Epochs of Chinese and Japanese Art*. 2 vols. New York: Dover Publications, Inc., 1921.

FIEDLER, CONRAD. *On Judging Works of Art*. Berkeley: University of California Press, 1949.

FLEXNER, JAMES T. *Pocket History of American Painting*. New York: Washington Square Press, Inc., 1962.

FOCILLON, HENRI. *The Life of Forms in Art*. New York: George Wittenborn, Inc., 1966.

FORTE, NANCY. *The Warrior in Art*. Minneapolis: Lerner Publications Co., 1965.

FRY, ROGER. *Cezanne*. New York: Macmillan Co., 1958.

GARDNER, HELEN. *Art Through the Ages*. 5th ed. New York: Harcourt, Brace & World, Inc., 1970.

GAUNT, WILLIAM. *A Concise History of English Painting*. New York: Praeger Publishers, Inc., 1967.

———. *Impressionism: A Visual History*. New York: Praeger Publishers, Inc., 1970.

GEZARI, TEMINA F. *Footprints and New Worlds: Experiences in Art with Child and Adult*. New York: Reconstructionist Press, 1957.

GIBSON, KATHERINE. *More Pictures to Grow Up With*. New York: Viking Press, Inc., 1942.

———. *Pictures by Young Americans*. New York: Oxford University Press, 1946.

GILL, ERIC. *Art and a Changing Civilization*. London: John Lane, The Bodley Head, 1934.

———. *Transformations*. New York: Doubleday & Co., Inc., 1956.

———. *Vision and Design*. New York: World Publishing Co., Meridian Books, 1956.

GLUBOK, SHIRLEY. *The Art of Ancient Egypt*. New York: Atheneum Publishers, 1962.

———. *The Art of Ancient Greece*. New York: Atheneum Publishers, 1963.

———. *The Art of Ancient Rome*. New York: Harper & Row, Publishers, 1965.

———. *The Art of the Eskimo*. New York: Harper & Row, Publishers, 1965.

———. *The Art of Lands in the Bible*. New York: Atheneum Publishers, 1963.

———. *The Art of the North American Indian*. New York: Harper & Row, Publishers, 1964.

*Golden Encyclopedia of Art*. New York: Western Publishing Co., Inc., Golden Press, 1961.

*Golden Book of the Renaissance*. New York: Western Publishing Co., Inc., Golden Press, 1962.

GOLDWATER, ROBERT. *Modern Art in Your Life*. New York: Museum of Modern Art, 1959.

———, and TREVES, MARCO. *Artists on Art*. 2nd ed. New York: Random House, Inc., Pantheon Books, Inc., 1947.

GOMBRICH, E. H. *Art and Illusion*. New York: Random House, Inc., Pantheon Books, Inc., 1960.

———. *The Story of Art*. London: Phaidon Press, 1962.

GOODRICH, LLOYD, and BAUR, JOHN. *American Art of Our Century*. New York: Praeger Publishers, Inc., 1961.

GRACZA, MARGARET YOUNG. *The Bird in Art*. Minneapolis: Lerner Publications Co., 1965.

———. *The Ship and the Sea in Art*. Minneapolis: Lerner Publications Co., 1964.

GROPIUS, WALTER. *The New Architecture*. Boston, Mass.: Charles T. Branford Co. Nd.

HAMLIN, TALBOT. *Architecture Through the Ages*. New York: G. P. Putnam's Sons, 1953.

HARKONEN, HELEN B. *Circuses and Fairs in Art*. Minneapolis: Lerner Publications Co., 1964.

———. *Farms and Farmers in Art*. Minneapolis: Lerner Publications Co., 1964.

HAYES, BARTLETT H., and RATHBURN, MARY. *A Layman's Guide to Modern Art*. New York: Oxford University Press, 1948.

HELFRITZ, HANS. *Mexican Cities of the Gods: An Archeological Guide*. New York: Praeger Publishers, Inc., 1970.

HEYNE, CARL, JR., et al. *Art for Young America*. Rev. ed. Peoria, Ill.: Chas. A. Bennett Co., Inc., 1970.

HIGGINS, REYNOLD. *Minoan and Mycenaean Art*. New York: Praeger Publishers, Inc., 1967.

HILLYER, V. M., and HUEY, E. G. *A Child's History of Art*. New York: Appleton-Century-Crofts, 1951.

HOLME, BRYAN. *Pictures to Live With*. New York: Viking Press, 1960.

HUNTER, SAM. *Modern French Painting*. New York: Dell Publishing Co., Inc., Nd.

HUYGHE, RENE. "Art and Mankind." *Larousse Encyclopedia of Prehistoric and Ancient Art*. New York: Prometheus, 1962.

HUMPHREYS, ALFRED. *Films on Art*. Washington, D. C.: The National Art Education Association, 1960.

———. *Index to 16mm Educational Films*. McGraw-Hill Book Co., 1967.

ITTEN, JOHANNES. *The Art of Color*. New York: Reinhold Publishing Corp., 1961.

———. *Design and Form: The Basic Course at the Bauhaus*. New York: Reinhold Publishing Corp., 1963.

JANSON, H. W. *Key Monuments of the History of Art*. Englewood Cliffs, N. J.: Prentice-Hall, Inc., and New York: Harry N. Abrams, Inc., 1959.

———. and JANSON, DORA JANE. *The Story of Painting for Young People*. New York: Harry N. Abrams, Inc., 1962.

KABLO, MARTIN. *World of Color*. New York: McGraw-Hill Book Co., 1963.

KAINZ, LOUISE, and RILEY, OLIVE. *Exploring Art*. New York: Harcourt, Brace & Co., Inc., 1947.

KAUFMANN, EDGAR. *What Is Modern Interior Design?* New York: Museum of Modern Art, 1958.

KEISLER, LEONARD. *Art is Everywhere*. New York: Dodd, Mead & Co., 1958.

———. *What's in a Line*. New York: Dodd, Mead & Co. 1962.

KELDER, DIANE. *The French Impressionists and Their Century*. New York: Praeger Publishers, Inc., 1970.

KEPES, GYORGY. *The Language of Vision*. Chicago: Theobald, 1945.

KIELTY, BERNARDINE. *Masters of Painting: Their Works, Their Lives, Their Times*. New York: Doubleday & Co., Inc., 1964.

KIRN, ANN. *Full of Wonder*. Cleveland: World Publishing Co., 1959.

KIRSTEN, LINCOLN. *The Sculpture of Elie Nadelman*. New York: Museum of Modern Art, 1948.

KNOBLER, NATHAN. *The Visual Dialogue*. New York: Holt, Rinehart & Winston, Inc., 1967.

KOESTLER, ARTHUR. *The Act of Creation*. New York: Macmillan Co., 1964.

KUH, KATHERINE. *Art Has Many Faces*. New York: Harper & Bros., 1951.

———. *The Artist's Voice*. New York: Harper & Row, Publishers, 1962.

LARKIN, OLIVER. *Art and Life in America*. New York: Holt, Rinehart & Winston, Inc., 1949.

LERNER, SHARON. *The Self-Portrait in Art*. Minneapolis: Lerner Publications Co., 1964.

LEVEY, MICHAEL. *A Concise History of Painting from Giotto to Cezanne*. New York: Praeger Publishers, Inc., 1962.

———. *A History of Western Art*. New York: Praeger Publishers, Inc., 1968.

LIBERMAN, ALEXANDER. *The Artist in His Studios*. New York: The Viking Press, 1960.

LINDERMAN, EARL W. *Invitation to Vision*. Dubuque, Ia.: Wm. C. Brown Co. Publishers, 1967.

LINGSTROM, FREDA. *The Seeing Eye*. New York: Macmillan Co., 1960.

LIPMAN, JEAN. *American Folk Art in Wood, Metal and Stone*. New York: Dover Publications Inc., Nd.

LIPPARD, LUCY R. *Pop Art*. New York: Praeger Publishers, Inc., 1966.

LOWRY, BATES. *The Visual Experience: An Introduction to Art*. Englewood Cliffs, N. J.: Prentice-Hall, Inc., 1967.

LUCIE-SMITH, EDWARD. *The Late Modern: Visual Arts Since 1945*. New York: Praeger Publishers, Inc., 1969.

LYNES, RUSSELL. *The Taste Makers*. New York: Harper & Bros., 1954.

MacAGY, DOUGLAS, and MacAGY, ELIZABETH. *Going for a Walk with a Line*. New York: Doubleday & Co., Inc., 1959.

McCURDY, CHARLES, ed. *Modern Art: A Pictorial Anthology*. New York: Macmillan Co., 1958.

McDARRAH, FRED W. *The Artist's World*. New York: E. P. Dutton & Co., Inc., 1961.

McKINNEY, ROLAND. *Famous French Painters*. New York: Dodd, Mead & Co., 1960.

MACQUOID, PERCY. *A History of English Furniture*. 4 vols. New York: Dover Publications Inc., 1968.

MARKS, ROBERT. *The Dymaxion World of Buckminster Fuller.* New York: Reinhold Publishing Corp., 1960.

MARTINDALE, ANDREW. *Gothic Art.* New York: Praeger Publishers, Inc., 1967.

MATHEY, FRANCOIS. *The Impressionists.* New York: Praeger Publishers, Inc., 1967.

MAYER, RALPH. *The Artist's Handbook of Materials and Techniques.* New York: Viking Press, 1945.

MEADER, ROBERT F. W. *Illustrated Guide to Shaker Furniture.* New York: Dover Publications, Inc., Nd.

MENDELOWITZ, DANIEL M. *A History of American Art.* New York: Holt, Rinehart & Winston, Inc., 1960.

MEYERS, BERNARD. *Understanding the Arts.* New York: Holt, Rinehart & Winston, Inc., 1963.

MOHOLY-NAGY, LASZLO. *Vision in Motion.* Chicago: Theobald, 1947.

MOORE, LAMONT. *The First Book of Architecture.* New York: Franklin Watts, Inc., 1961.

———. *The First Book of Paintings.* New York: Franklin Watts, Inc., 1960.

MULLER, JOSEPH-EMILE. *Fauvism.* Translated by Shirley Jones. New York: Praeger Publishers, Inc., 1967.

MUNRO, ELEANOR. *The Golden Encyclopedia of Art.* New York: McGraw-Hill Book Co., 1967.

MURRAY, LINDA. *High Renaissance.* New York: Praeger Publishers, Inc., 1967.

———. *The Late Renaissance and Mannerism.* New York: Praeger Publishers, Inc., 1967.

MYERS, BERNARD S. *Art and Civilization.* 2nd ed. New York: McGraw-Hill Book Co., 1967.

———. *Modern Art in the Making.* New York: McGraw-Hill Book Co., 1959.

———. *Understanding the Arts.* New York: Holt, Rinehart & Winston, Inc., 1959.

NAIRN, IAN. *The American Landscape: A Critical View.* New York: Random House, Inc., 1965.

NATIONAL CULTURAL CENTER. *Creative America.* Washington, D. C.: Ridge Press, Inc., 1962.

NEUTRA, RICHARD. *Life and Shape.* New York: Appleton-Century-Crofts, 1962.

———. *Survival Through Design.* Oxford, N.Y.: Harper, 1952.

NICHOLAS, NEYNE, LEE, TRILLING. *Art for Young America.* Peoria: Charles A. Bennett Co., 1960.

NORBERG-SCHULTZ, CHRISTIAN. *Existence, Space, and Architecture.* New York: Praeger Publishers, Inc., 1971.

NUGENT, FRANCES ROBERT. *Jan Van Eyck—Master Painter.* New York: Rand McNally & Co., 1962.

OCVIRK, OTTO; BONE, ROBERT; STINSON, ROBERT; and WIGG, PHILIP. *Art Fundamentals.* Dubuque, Ia.: Wm. C. Brown Co. Publishers, 1962.

OERI, GEORGINE. *Man and His Images.* New York: Viking Press, Inc., 1968.

OGDEN, C. K.; RICHARDS, I. A.; and WOOD, JAMES. *The Foundation of Aesthetics.* New York: International Publishers Co., Inc., 1931.

ORPEN, WILLIAM. *The Outline of Art.* New York: Transatlantic Arts, Inc., 1955.

PEPPER, STEPHEN. *The Basis of Criticism in the Arts.* Cambridge, Mass.: Harvard University Press, 1941.

PHILLIPS, LISLE MARCH. *The Work of Man.* London: Duckworth, 1956.

POLLACK, PETER. *The Picture History of Photography.* New York: Harry N. Abrams, Inc., 1958.

*Praeger Picture Encyclopedia of Art.* New York: Frederick A. Praeger Co., 1958.

PRICE, CHRISTINE. *Made in the Middle Ages.* New York: E. P. Dutton & Co., Inc., 1961.

RADER, MELVIN. *A Modern Book of Aesthetics.* New York: Holt, Rinehart & Winston, Inc., 1951.

RASMUSEN, HENRY. *Art Structure.* New York: McGraw-Hill Book Co., 1950.

READ, SIR HERBERT. *Art and Industry.* New York: Horizon Press, 1961.

———. *A Concise History of Modern Painting.* Rev. ed. New York: Praeger Publishers, Inc., 1969.

———. *Surrealism.* Reprint of 1936 ed. Elmsford, N.Y.: British Book Center, 1971.

———. *A Concise History of Modern Sculpture.* New York: Praeger Publishers, Inc., 1964.

———. *Art Now.* 2nd ed. New York: Pitman Publishing Corp., 1960.

———. *The Grass Roots of Art.* New York: World Publishing Co., 1961.

———. *The Meaning of Art.* 3rd ed. Baltimore: Penguin Books, Inc., 1959.

REID, LOUIS A. *A Study in Aesthetics.* New York: Macmillan Co., 1931.

REUSCH, JURGEN, and KEES, WELDON. *Nonverbal Communication*. Berkeley: University of California Press, 1956.

RICE, DAVID TALBOT. *Islamic Art*. New York: Praeger Publishers, Inc., 1965.

———. *A Concise History of Painting from Prehistory to the Thirteenth Century*. New York: Praeger Publishers, Inc., 1968.

RICE, TAMARA TALBOT. *A Concise History of Russian Art*. New York: Praeger Publishers, Inc., 1963.

RICHTER, GISELA M. *Handbook of Greek Art*. 6th ed. New York: Praeger Publishers, Inc., Phaidon Press Art Books, 1969.

RICHTER, HANS. *Dada: Art and Anti-Art*. New York: Harry N. Abrams, Inc., 1970.

RILEY, OLIVE. *Masks and Magic*. New York: Studio-Crowell, 1955.

RIPLEY, ELIZABETH. *Botticelli: A Biography*. New York: J. B. Lippincott Co., 1960.

———. *Durer*. Philadelphia: J. B. Lippincott Co., 1958.

———. *Goya*, New York: Henry Z. Walck, Inc., 1956.

———. *Leonardo da Vinci*. New York: Henry Z. Walck, Inc., 1952.

———. *Rembrandt*. New York: Henry Z. Walck, Inc., 1955.

———. *Rubens*. New York: Henry Z. Walck, Inc., 1957.

RITCHIE, ANDREW. *Sculpture of the Twentieth Century*. New York: Museum of Modern Art, 1958.

ROBB, DAVID M., and GARRISON, J. J. *Art in the Western World*. New York: Harper & Row, Publishers, 1965.

ROOS, FRANK J., JR. *An Illustrated Handbook of Art History*. 3rd ed. New York: Macmillan Co., 1970.

ROSE, BARBARA. *The Golden Age of Dutch Painting*. New York: Praeger Publishers, Inc., 1969.

ROWLAND, KURT. *Learning to See*. 5 books. New York: Van Nostrand Reinhold Co., 1971.

| | |
|---|---|
| G7094-0001 | *Learning to See* 1 |
| G7097-0008 | *Learning to See* 1 Workbook |
| G7100-0002 | *Learning to See* 1 Teacher's Book |
| G7095-0007 | *Learning to See* 2 |
| G7098-0003 | *Learning to See* 2 Workbook |
| G7101-0008 | *Learning to See* 2 Teacher's Book |
| G7096-0002 | *Learning to See* 3 |
| G7099-0009 | *Learning to See* 3 Workbook |
| G7102-0003 | *Learning to See* 3 Teacher's Book |
| G7108-0006 | *Learning to See* 4 |
| G7110-0007 | *Learning to See* 4 Workbook |
| G7111-0002 | *Learning to See* 4 Teacher's Book |
| G7112-0008 | *Learning to See* 5 |
| G7114-0009 | *Learning to See* 5 Teacher's Book |

———. Looking and Seeing series. 4 vols. New York: Van Nostrand Reinhold Co.

| | |
|---|---|
| G7086-0008 | *Pattern and Shape*. Vol. 1, 1964. |
| G7087-0003 | *Pattern and Shape*. Note for Teachers, 1964. |
| G7088-0009 | *The Development of Shape*. Vol. 2. |
| G7089-0004 | *The Development of Shape*. Notes for Teachers. |
| G7090-000x | *The Shapes We Need*. Vol. 3, 1965. |
| G7091-0005 | *The Shapes We Need*. Notes for Teachers, 1965. |
| G7092-0000 | The *Shape of Towns*. Vol. 4, 1966. |
| G7093-0006 | *The Shape of Towns*. Notes for Teachers, 1966. |

Slides are available to accompany the four volumes of Looking and Seeing. Please ask for information and order form from Van Nostrand Reinhold Co.

ROSENBERG, HAROLD. *The Anxious Object: Art Today and Its Audience*. New York: Horizon Press, 1964.

RUBIN, WILLIAM S. *Dada, Surrealism and Their Heritage*. New York: Museum of Modern Art, 1968.

RUDOFSKY, BERNARD. *Architecture Without Architects*. New York: Museum of Modern Art, 1964.

RUNES, DAGOBERT, and SCHRICKEL, HARRY D. *Encyclopedia of the Arts*. New York: Philosophical Society, 1946.

RUSKIN, ARIANE. *Story of Art for Young People*. New York: Pantheon Books, Inc., 1964.

RUSSELL, JOHN, and GABLIK, SUZI. *Pop Art Redefined*. New York: Praeger Publishers, Inc., 1969.

SACHS, PAUL J. *Modern Prints and Drawings*. New York: Alfred A. Knopf, Inc., 1954.

SCHAEFER-SIMMERN, HENRY. *The Unfolding of Artistic Activity: Its Basis, Processes and Implications*. Berkeley and Los Angeles, Calif.: University of California Press, 1948.

SCHINNELLER, JAMES A. *Art: Search and Self-Discovery*. 2nd ed. Scranton, Pa.: International Textbook, 1968.

SCHORR, JUSTIN. *Aspects of Art*. Cranbury, N. J.: A. S. Barnes & Co., Inc., 1967.

SCHWARTZ, PAUL W. *Cubism*. New York: Praeger Publishers, Inc., 1971.

SEIBERLING, FRANK. *Looking Into Art*, New York: Holt, Rinehart & Winston, Inc., 1959.

SEITZ, WILLIAM CHAPIN. *The Art of the Assemblage*. New York: Museum of Modern Art, 1965.

———. *The Responsive Eye*. New York: Museum of Modern Art, 1965.

SEUPHOR, MICHEL. *Sculpture of This Century*. New York: George Braziller, Inc., 1960.

SEWALL, JOHN IVES. *A History of Western Art*. New York: Holt, Rinehart & Winston, Inc., 1963.

SHAHN, BEN. *The Shape of Content*. Cambridge, Mass.: Harvard University Press, 1957.

SIMON, CHARLIE MAY. *Art in the New Land*. New York: E. P. Dutton & Co., Inc., 1954.

SIMPSON, MARTHA. *Art Is for Everyone*. New York: McGraw-Hill Book Co., 1951.

*Skira Art Portfolios*. Cleveland, O.: World Publishing Co., Skira Art Books.

SMITH, RALPH. *Aesthetics and Criticism in Art Education, Problems in Defining, Explaining and Evaluating Art*. Chicago: Rand McNally & Co., 1966.

SPENCER, CORNELIA. *How Art and Music Speak to Us*. New York: John Day, 1963.

STEER, JOHN. *A Concise History of Venetian Painting*. New York: Praeger Publishers, Inc., 1970.

SULLIVAN, LOUIS. *The Autobiography of an Idea*. New York: Dover Publications, Inc., 1956.

TAYLOR, HAROLD. *Art and the Intellect*. New York: Museum of Modern Art, 1960.

TAYLOR, JOSHUA C. *Learning to Look: A Handbook for the Visual Arts*. Chicago: University of Chicago Press, 1957.

UPJOHN, EVERARD; WINGERT, PAUL; and MAHLER, JUNE. *History of World Art*. New York: Oxford University Press, 1949.

WARD, A. C. *Enjoying Paintings*. London, England: Phoenix House Publishers. Nd.

WATERHOUSE, ELLIS. *Italian Baroque Painting*. Rev. ed. New York: Praeger Publishers, Inc., Phaidon Press Books, 1970.

WECHSLER, HERMAN J. *The Pocket Book of Old Masters*. New York: Washington Square Press, Inc., 1961.

WEISGARD, LEONARD. *Treasures to See*. New York: Harcourt, Brace & World, Inc., 1956.

WHEELER, MONROE. *Modern Drawings*. New York: Museum of Modern Art, 1944.

WHEELER, MORTIMER. *Roman Art and Architecture*. New York: Praeger Publishers, Inc., 1964.

WHITNEY, ELWOOD. *Symbology: The Use of Symbols in Visual Communication*. New York: Hastings House, 1960.

WRIGHT, FRANK LLOYD. *The Living City*. New York: Horizon Press, 1958.

ZUCKER, PAUL. *Styles in Painting*. New York: Viking Press, Inc., 1950.

ZUELKE, RUTH. *The Horse in Art*. Minneapolis: Lerner Publications Co., 1965.

Harry N. Abrams, Inc., 110 E. 59 St., New York, N.Y. 10022.
American Book Co., 450 W. 33 St., New York, N.Y. 10001; 300 Pike St., Cincinnati, Ohio 45202.
The Antioch Press, Kent State University Press, Kent, Ohio 44240.
Apollo Editions, Inc., 666 Fifth Ave., New York, N.Y. 10019.
Appleton-Century-Crofts, 440 Park Ave. S., New York, N.Y. 10016.
Architectural Book Pub. Co., Inc., 10 E. 40th St., New York, N.Y. 10016.
Avon Book Div., The Hearst Corp., 959 Eighth Ave., New York, N.Y. 10019.

Ballantine Books, Inc., 101 Fifth Ave., New York, N.Y. 10003.
Bantam Books, Inc., 666 Fifth Ave., New York, N.Y. 10019.
Barnes & Noble Books, 10 E. 53 St., New York, N.Y. 10022.
Barron's Educational Series, Inc., 113 Crossways Park Dr., Woodbury, N.Y. 11797.
Basic Books, Inc., 10 E. 53 St., New York, N.Y. 10022.
The Beacon Press, 25 Beacon St., Boston, Mass. 02108.
Bloch Publishing Co., Inc., 915 Broadway, New York, N.Y. 10010.
The Bobbs-Merrill Co., 4300 W. 62nd St., Indianapolis, Ind. 46268.
The Book House for Children, United Educators, Inc., Lake Bluff, Ill. 60044.
Wm. C. Brown Company Publishers, 2460 Kerper Blvd., Dubuque, Iowa 52001.
Burgess Publishing Co., 426 Sixth St., Minneapolis, Minn. 55415.

California Test Bureau, Del Monte Research Park, Monterey, Calif. 93940.
Cambridge Univ. Press, 32 E. 57th St., New York, N.Y. 10022.
The Caxton Printers, Ltd., 312 Main St., Caldwell, Idaho 83605.
Chelsea Publishing Co., Inc., 159 E. Tremont Ave., Bronx, N.Y. 10453.
Chicago Natural History Museum, Roosevelt Rd. and Lake Shore Dr., Chicago, Ill. 60605.
The Child's World, Inc., Creative Educational Soc., Inc., 515 N. Front St., Mankato, Minn. 56001.
Childrens Press, Inc., 1224 W. Van Buren St., Chicago, Ill. 60607.
College Art Association of America, 432 Park Ave. S., New York, N.Y. 10016.
P. F. Collier, Inc., 866 3rd Ave., New York, N.Y. 10022.
Wm. Collins Sons & Co., Ltd., 215 Park Ave. S., New York, N.Y. 10003.
Columbia Univ. Press, 562 W. 113th St., New York, N.Y. 10025.
Cornell Univ. Press, 124 Roberts Pl., Ithaca, N.Y. 14850.
Creative Educational Society, 515 North Front St., Mankato, Minn. 56001.
Criterion Books, 257 Park Ave. S., New York, N.Y. 10010.
Thomas Y. Crowell Co., 666 Fifth Ave., New York, N.Y. 10009.
Crown Publishers, 419 Park Ave. S., New York, N.Y. 10016.

Davis Publications, Inc., 229 Park Ave. S., New York, N.Y. 10003.
Dell Publishing Co., Inc., 750 Third Ave., New York, N.Y. 10017.
Delmar Publishers, Mountainview Ave., Albany, N.Y. 12205.
Dodd, Mead and Co., 79 Madison Ave., New York, N.Y. 10016.
Doubleday & Co., Inc., 277 Park Ave., Garden City, N.Y. 10017.
Dover Publications, Inc., 180 Varick St., New York, N.Y. 10014.
Duke Univ. Press, College Station, Box 6697, Durham, N.C. 27708.
E. P. Dutton & Co., Inc., 201 Park Ave. S., New York, N.Y. 10003.

J. W. Edwards, Publisher, Inc., 2500 S. State St., Ann Arbor, Mich. 48104.
Encyclopaedia Britannica, Inc., 425 N. Michigan Ave., Chicago, Ill. 60611.
Expression Co., Publishers, P.O. Box 11, Magnolia, Mass. 01930.

Fawcett World Library: Crest, Gold Medal & Premier Books, 1 Astor Plaza, New York, N.Y. 10036.
Field Enterprises Educational Corp., 510 Merchandise Mart Plaza, Chicago, Ill. 60654.

Follett Publishing Co., 1010 W. Washington Blvd., Chicago, Ill. 60607.
Fordham Univ. Press, 411 E. Fordham Rd., Bronx, N.Y. 10458.
W. H. Freeman and Co. Publishers, 660 Market St., San Francisco, Calif. 94104.
Samuel French, Inc., 25 W. 45th St., New York, N.Y. 10036.
Funk & Wagnalls Publishing Co., 666 Fifth Ave., New York, N.Y. 10019.

Ginn & Co., 191 Spring St., Lexington, Mass. 02173.
Glenco Press, 8701 Wilshire Blvd., Beverly Hills, Calif. 90211.
Golden Press, Inc., 1220 Mound Ave., Racine, Wis. 53404.
Grosset & Dunlap, Inc., 51 Madison Ave., New York, N.Y. 10010.
Grove Press, Inc., 53 E. 11 St., New York, N.Y. 10003.

Harcourt Brace Jovanovich, Inc., 757 Third Ave., New York, N.Y. 10017.
Harlem Book Co., Tudor Pub. Co., 572 Fifth Ave., New York, N.Y. 10036.
Harlow Publishing Corp., 212 E. Grey, Norman, Oklahoma 73069.
Harper & Row, Publishers, 10 E. 53 St., New York, N.Y. 10022.
Harvard Univ. Press, 79 Garden St., Cambridge, Mass. 02138.
Hastings House, Publishers, Inc., 10 E. 40 St., New York, N.Y. 10016.
W. S. Heinman, Imported Books, 200 W. 72 St., New York, N.Y. 10023.
Holt, Rinehart & Winston, Inc., 383 Madison Ave., New York, N.Y. 10017.
Houghton Mifflin Co., 2 Park St., Boston, Mass. 02107.
Humanities Press, Inc., 303 Park Ave. S., New York, N.Y. 10010.
Hutchins Oriental Books, P.O. Box 177, 1603 Hope St., South Pasadena, Calif. 91031.

Indiana Univ. Press, 10th and Morton Sts., Bloomington, Ind. 47401.
International Publishers Co., Inc., 381 Park Ave. S., New York, N.Y. 10016.
International Textbook Co., Intex Educational Publishers, Scranton, Pa. 18515.
International Universities Press, 239 Park Ave. S., New York, N.Y. 10003.
Iowa State Univ. Press, Ames, Iowa 50010.

The Johns Hopkins Univ. Press, Baltimore, Md. 21218.

Alfred A. Knopf, Inc., 201 E. 50 St., New York, N.Y. 10022.

Liberal Arts Press, Inc., 4300 W. 62nd St., Indianapolis, Ind. 46268.
J. B. Lippincott Co., E. Washington Square, Philadelphia, Pa. 19105.
Little, Brown & Co., 34 Beacon St., Boston, Mass. 02106.
Louisiana State Univ. Press, Hill Memorial Bldg., Louisiana State Univ., Baton Rouge, La. 70803.
Loyola Univ. Press, 3441 N. Ashland Ave., Chicago, Ill. 60657.
Lyons & Carnahan, 407 E. 25 St., Chicago, Ill. 60616

McGraw-Hill Book Co., Inc., 1221 Ave. of the Americas, New York, N.Y. 10020.
The Macmillan Co., 866 Third Ave., New York, N.Y. 10022.
David McKay Co., Inc., 750 Third Ave., New York, N.Y. 10017.
McKnight & McKnight Pub. Co., U.S. Route 66 at Towanda Ave., Bloomington, Ill. 61701.
Meredith Press, Div. of Meredith Pub. Co., 1716 Locust St., Des Moines, Iowa 50336.
Meridian Books, Inc., World Publishing Co., 110 E. 59 St., New York, N.Y. 10022.
Charles E. Merrill Publishing Co., 1300 Alum Creek Drive, Columbus, Ohio 43216.
Michigan State Univ. Press, Box 550, E. Lansing, Mich. 48823.
M.I.T. Press, 28 Carleton St., Cambridge, Mass. 02142.
Modern Library, Inc., 201 E. 50 St., New York, N.Y. 10022.
Monarch Press, 630 Fifth Ave., New York, N.Y. 10020.

National Art Education Association, 1201 16th St., N.W., Washington, D.C. 20036.
New American Library, Inc., 1301 Ave. of the Americas, New York, N.Y. 10019.
New York Graphic Society Ltd., 140 Greenwich Ave., Greenwich, Conn. 06830.
New York Univ. Press, Washington Sq., New York, N.Y. 10003.
Noble & Noble, Pub., Inc., 750 Third Ave., New York, N.Y. 10017.
Northwestern Univ. Press, 1735 Benson, Evanston, Ill. 60201.
W. W. Norton & Co., Inc., 55 Fifth Ave., New York, N.Y. 10003.

The Odyssey Press, 4300 W. 62 St., Indianapolis, Ind. 46268.
Ohio State Univ. Press, 2070 Neil Ave., Columbus, Ohio 43210.
Oxford Univ. Press, 200 Madison Ave., New York, N.Y. 10016.

Pantheon Books, Inc., 201 E. 50 St., New York, N.Y. 10022.
Parents' Magazine's Educational Press, Div. of Parents' Magazine's Enterprises, Inc., 52 Vanderbilt Ave., New York, N.Y. 10017.
Penguin Books, Inc., 7110 Ambassador Rd., Baltimore, Md. 21207.
Pergamon Press, Inc., Maxwell House, Fairview Park, Elmsford, N.Y. 10523.
Pitman Publishing Corp., 6 E. 43 St., New York, N.Y. 10017.
Pocket Books, 630 Fifth Ave., New York, N.Y. 10020.
Popular Library, 355 Lexington Ave., New York, N.Y. 10017.
Praeger Publishers, Inc., 111 Fourth Ave., New York, N.Y. 10003.
Prentice-Hall Inc., Englewood Cliffs, N.J. 07632.
Princeton Univ. Press, Princeton, N.J. 08540.
The Psychological Corp., 304 E. 45 St., New York, N.Y. 10017.
G. P. Putnam's Sons, 200 Madison Ave., New York, N.Y. 10016.
Pyramid Publications, Inc., 444 Madison Ave., New York, N.Y. 10022.

Quadrangle Books, Inc., 330 Madison Ave., New York, N.Y., 10017.

Rand McNally & Co., Box 7600, Chicago, Ill. 60680.
Random House, Inc., 201 E. 50 St., New York, N.Y. 10022.
Reader's Digest Services, Inc., Pleasantville, N.Y. 10570.

St. Martin's Press, Inc., 175 Fifth Ave., New York, N.Y. 10010.
Scholastic Book Services, 50 W. 44 St., New York, N.Y. 10036.
Charles Scribner's Sons, 597 Fifth Ave., New York, N.Y. 10017.
Silver Burdett Co., General Learning Corp., 250 James St., Morristown, N.J. 07960.
Simon & Schuster, Inc., 630 Fifth Ave., New York, N.Y. 10020.
Skira Art Books, 110 E. 59 St., New York, N.Y. 10022.
Southern Illinois Univ. Press, Box 697, Carbondale, Ill. 62901.
Southern Methodist Univ. Press, Dallas, Texas 75222.
South-Western Publishing Co., 5101 Madison Rd., Cincinnati, Ohio 45227.
Stanford Univ. Press, Stanford, Calif. 94305.
The Superintendent of Documents, U.S. Government Printing Office, Washington, D.C. 20402.
Syracuse Univ. Press, University Station, Box 8, Syracuse, N.Y. 13210.

Teachers College Press, Columbia Univ., 1234 Amsterdam Ave., New York, N.Y. 10027.
Theatre Arts Books, 333 Ave. of the Americas, New York, N.Y. 10014.
Charles C Thomas, Publisher, 301-327 E. Lawrence Ave., Springfield, Ill. 62703.

The United Educators, Inc., Tangley Oaks Educational Center, Lake Bluff, Ill. 60044.
United Nations, Sales Section, Room 1059, New York, N.Y. 10017.
University Books, Inc., 1615 Hillside Ave., New Hyde Park, N.Y. 11041.
Univ. of Alabama Press, Mail Drawer 2877, University, Alabama 35486.
Univ. of California Press, 2223 Fulton St., Berkeley, Calif. 94720.
Univ. of Chicago Press, 5801 Ellis Ave., Chicago, Ill. 60637.
Univ. of Florida Press, 15 N.W. 15th St., Gainesville, Fla. 32601.
Univ. of Georgia Press, Athens, Ga. 30601.
Univ. of Illinois Press, Urbana, Ill. 61801.
Univ. of Miami Press, P.O. Drawer 9088, Coral Gables, Fla. 33124.

Univ. of Michigan Press, Ann Arbor, Mich. 48106.
Univ. of Minnesota Press, 2037 University Ave. S.E., Minneapolis, Minn. 55455.
Univ. of Nebraska Press, 901 N. 17th St., Lincoln, Nebr. 68508.
Univ. of New Mexico Press, Journalism 220, Albuquerque, N.M. 87106.
Univ. of North Carolina Press, Box 2288, Chapel Hill, N.C. 27514.
Univ. of Notre Dame Press, Notre Dame, Ind. 46556.
Univ. of Oklahoma Press, 1005 Asp Ave., Norman, Okla. 73069.
Univ. of Pennsylvania Press, 3933 Walnut St., Philadelphia, Pa. 19104.
Univ. of Pittsburgh Press, 127 N. Bellefield Ave., Pittsburgh, Pa. 15213.
University Society, Inc., 25 Cottage St., Midland Park, N.J. 07432.
Univ. of South Carolina Press, Columbia, S.C. 29208.
Univ. of Tennessee Press, Communications Bldg., Knoxville, Tenn. 37916.
Univ. of Texas Press, Box 7819 Univ. Sta., Austin, Texas 78712.
Univ. of Washington Press, Seattle, Wash. 98105.
Univ. of Wisconsin Press, P.O. Box 1379, Madison, Wis. 53701.
Univ. Press of Hawaii, 535 Ward Ave., Honolulu, Hawaii 96814.
Univ. Press of Kansas, 358 Watson Lby., Lawrence, Kansas 66044.
Univ. Press of Kentucky, Lexington, Ky. 40506.
Univ. Press of Washington, D.C., Suite 321, 1010 Vermont Ave., N.W., Washington,
    D.C. 20005.


Van Nostrand Reinhold Co., 450 W. 33 St., New York, N.Y. 10001.
Vanderbilt Univ. Press, Kirkland Hall, Nashville, Tenn. 37235.
Vanguard Press, Inc., 424 Madison Ave., New York, N.Y. 10017.
The Viking Press, Inc., 625 Madison Ave., New York, N.Y. 10022.
Vintage Books, Inc., 201 E. 50 St., New York, N.Y. 10022.


Wadsworth Publishing Co., Inc., Belmont, Calif. 94002.
Frederick Warne & Co., Inc., 101 Fifth Ave., New York, N.Y. 10003.
Watson-Guptill Publications, 165 W. 46th St., New York, N.Y. 10036.
Wayne State Univ. Press, 5980 Cass Ave., Detroit, Mich. 48202.
Wesleyan Univ. Press, 100 Riverview Ctr., Middletown, Conn. 06457.
Western Reserve Univ. Press, Quail Bldg., Cleveland, Ohio 44106.
John Wiley and Sons, Inc., 605 Third Ave., New York, N.Y. 10016.
The World Publishing Co., 110 E. 59th St., New York, N.Y. 10022.


Xerox College Publishing, 191 Spring St., Lexington, Mass. 02173.


Yale Univ. Press, 149 York St., New Haven, Conn. 06511.

# index

Italicized numbers indicate pages on which illustrations appear.